THE SOO LINE'S
FAMOUS TRAINS
TO CANADA

★ ★ ★

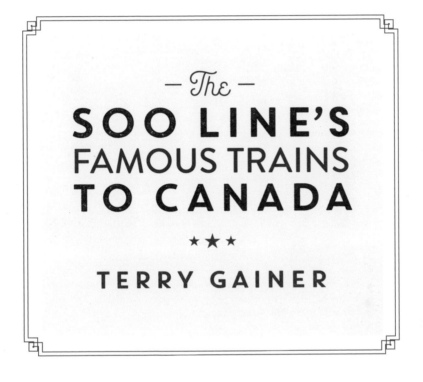

The

SOO LINE'S
FAMOUS TRAINS
TO CANADA

★ ★ ★

TERRY GAINER

RMB

For information on purchasing bulk quantities of this book, or to obtain media excerpts or invite the author to speak at an event, please visit rmbooks.com and select the "Contact" tab.

RMB | Rocky Mountain Books Ltd.
rmbooks.com
@rmbooks
facebook.com/rmbooks

Cataloguing data available from Library and Archives Canada
ISBN 9781771606714 (softcover)
ISBN 9781771606721 (electronic)

Design: Lara Minja, Lime Design

Cover image: A 1952 promotional shot of the Mountaineer at Morant's Curve. Photographer Nicholas Morant. Courtesy Whyte Museum of the Canadian Rockies and Archives.

Printed and bound in China

We would like to also take this opportunity to acknowledge the traditional territories upon which we live and work. In Calgary, Alberta, we acknowledge the Niitsítapi (Blackfoot) and the people of the Treaty 7 region in Southern Alberta, which includes the Siksika, the Piikuni, the Kainai, the Tsuut'ina, and the Stoney Nakoda First Nations, including Chiniki, Bearpaw, and Wesley First Nations. The City of Calgary is also home to Métis Nation of Alberta, Region III. In Victoria, British Columbia, we acknowledge the traditional territories of the Lkwungen (Esquimalt and Songhees), Malahat, Pacheedaht, Scia'new, T'Sou-ke, and W̱SÁNEĆ (Pauquachin, Tsartlip, Tsawout, Tseycum) peoples.

We acknowledge the financial support of the Government of Canada through the Canada Book Fund and the Canada Council for the Arts, and of the province of British Columbia through the British Columbia Arts Council and the Book Publishing Tax Credit.

IF WE CAN'T EXPORT THE SCENERY,
WE'LL IMPORT THE TOURISTS.

—**William Cornelius Van Horne,** President and Chairman,
Board of Directors, Canadian Pacific Railway

—— • ——

THE PASSENGER TRAIN IS LIKE THE MALE TEAT,
NEITHER USEFUL NOR ORNAMENTAL.

—**James J. Hill,** Founder and President, Great Northern Railway

— Contents —

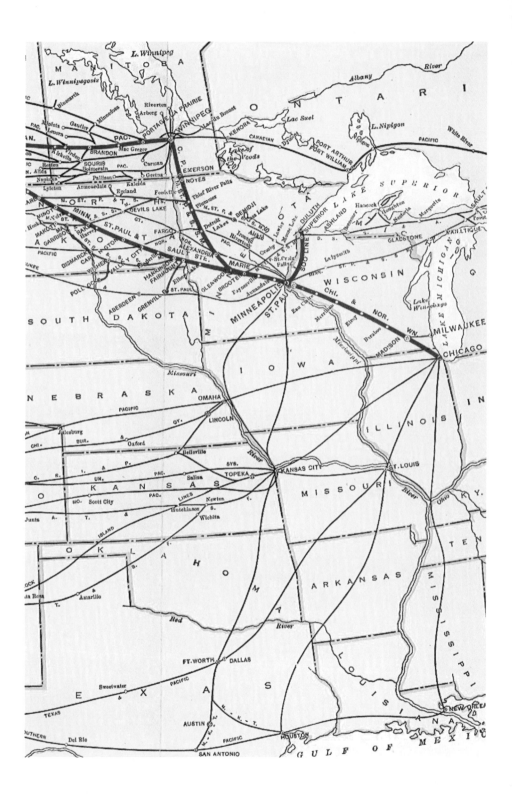

❧ FOREWORD ❧

Darryl Raymaker

TERRY GAINER modestly refers to himself as a "well-travelled vagabond." By definition, a *vagabond* is a person who moves from place to place without a fixed home, is unsettled, irresponsible, and, most often, disreputable.

I have known him for some 60 years, and I can assure the reader Gainer is no wandering, irresponsible vagrant, and neither is he disreputable. A soldier of fortune, perhaps, an adventurer for sure, and above all, a nonpareil storyteller. Whether at a book launch, boardroom, or as a dinner or luncheon companion, he entertains his audience with his formidable memory and grasp of detail, with the natural advantage of his inherited Irish wit. He likes to regale his listeners on all subjects, whether it be anecdotes of his youth, his travels, his variety of jobs, or his life experiences. He is a multitalented gentleman and is razor-sharp. Fortunately, he also writes the same way.

He has had some 50 years of executive management experience in all aspects of the hospitality and travel industries, including media relations and marketing. He has consulted on domestic and international projects and has served in executive capacities in motor coach transportation and rail companies. His work has also included business relationships with the US National Park Service and Parks Canada, and the tourism industry in Japan, New Zealand, Australia, the United States, and the United Kingdom.

But his muse is his beloved trains. Moving westward with his family to the jewel of the Canadian Rockies in Banff, Alberta, was an event that became the epiphany for his wanderlust for adventure. His father had taken the job as a station agent in Banff in 1948, and the family lived in quarters above the station. Terry was 6 years old.

He travelled the trains of Western Canada with his family, hung out at the station in Banff with his pals, picked up the basics of Morse code, and watched the activities of the switch crews and baggage handlers. He paid attention to maps charting passenger routes across Canada and the US and learned how to read voluminous train schedules. To Terry, Banff was the centre of the universe, with eight to ten passenger train arrivals daily, carrying folks from all corners of the world to some of the finest scenery this side of heaven.

When he was old enough to work in 1957, Canadian Pacific (CP) hired him for the summer to work in the baggage room, and his romance with trains became even more intense. A couple of years later, he became a redcap. Redcaps were responsible for loading and unloading the trains, finding lost or misdirected luggage, or directing the travellers to hotels, points of interest, where to dine, and other tourist needs. He learned how tour companies operated and prospered, easily relating to the tour managers accompanying the guests. His railway knowledge is legion: the history of trains, railroad entrepreneurs and corporate executives, the routes of the great North American railway companies, the various types of railway cars – the Pullmans, observation, and the posh cars of its corporate executives or high-rolling tourists. He also learned about the partnerships of railroad companies and the integration of their operations in their efforts to cover more market areas of cities and national parks in the United States and Canada, together with the extensive advertising programs designed to lure tourists and travellers into travelling by rail. But by the 1960s, the glory days of train travel ended. However, Terry's interest in tourism served him well, providing the basis for his professional career.

In recent years he has devoted a good deal of his time to sharing his knowledge of the romance of trains with the reading public. In 2019, he published his first book, *When Trains Ruled the Rockies: My Life at the Banff Railway Station*, wherein he describes his early years. The Canadian Pacific Railway (CPR) passed through Banff and was Canada's first trans-continental railway, leading to the spawning of the Canadian Rockies as a major tourist destination. When Hollywood, through the efforts of the Canadian Pacific Railway, discovered Banff and its scenery, a young Terry observed the filming of *Canadian Pacific*, a Randolph Scott western that featured a Hollywood version of the construction of the railway through the Rockies. He writes about gradually learning the ropes about railroads. By 1959, he had reached his nirvana of becoming a redcap, where he learned first-hand about the intricacies of front-line employees of the railroads (by the way, the tips were excellent). The book's ending coincides with the disappearance of rail travel.

It was followed shortly in 2022 by *When Trains Ruled the Kootenays: A Short History of Railways in Southeastern British Columbia*, which was the history of the transportation routes that served the mining industry and residents of southeastern British Columbia in the 20th century, and the competitive corporate action that was part of the game.

This is Terry's third effort: *The Soo Line's Famous Trains to Canada*. Here, he takes us back to the ice age and the Indigenous Peoples of the Dakota and Ojibwe. They were the original occupants of the lands surrounding Saint Paul and Minneapolis, the focus of his latest saga. The Dakota and the Ojibwe lived, hunted, and fished throughout present-day Minnesota for thousands of years and regarded the lands as sacred. He briefly takes us through the period of the early settlements of the area from 1825 to 1867, which relied on logging, farming, and milling of wheat.

In 1883, a group of Minneapolis local millers were tired of the Chicago railways charging extravagant freight rates to get their product to the eastern seaboard ports. They decided to form a new railway offering a different route, bypassing Chicago. The new railway was called the Minneapolis, Sault Ste. Marie & Atlantic Railway, more commonly called the Soo Line ("Soo" is an abbreviation for Sault Ste. Marie, Ontario). The new train service would leave Saint Paul station (Saint Paul is just across the river from Minneapolis, and together they are known as the "Twin Cities") and join the Canadian Pacific line at Sault Ste. Marie, Ontario, then proceed to Montreal on CP, then into the US on the Boston and Lowell line (a CP partner), and on to the ports of Boston and New York, where the product would be bound for world markets.

Charles Pillsbury of C.A. Pillsbury and Company (of Pillsbury Doughboy mascot fame), known as "the Largest Flour Mill in the World," and W.A. Washburn, a prominent miller and politician, provided the financial backing for the new venture.

The Canadian Pacific Railway took a controlling interest in the new Soo Line in the 1880s when the initial investors floundered. With control of the Soo, Canadian Pacific entered the US market. This provided CP with competitive strength in dealing with the cutthroat competition of the robber barons of the US railways. The Soo launched passenger trains from Chicago and the Twin Cities in head-on competition with the western expansion of the Great Northern Railway and competitive trains to the east coast.

Terry writes about this episode of North American railroad history with great zeal, particularly as regards the rancorous schism that broke out in 1883 between the leading CP executives and their American partner, railway entrepreneur James J. Hill of Great Northern, causing Hill to bail out of the syndicate and concentrate on Great Northern. The battles between Great Northern and CP for market share erupted from North Dakota to Western Canada for the next 30 years.

The Soo would introduce Americans to Montreal, Quebec City, the Canadian Rockies, and Vancouver, home port for CP's Pacific steamship service, and vied for passengers on its Spokane and Portland routes from the Twin Cities to the Pacific Northwest. In 1923, the Soo Line launched the Soo Mountaineer, the longest two-nation train journey in North America. Initially, the Soo Line was built to serve the agricultural industry. Still, it also became a leader in promoting passenger service for many thousands from the US to Canada's east and west coasts, feeding the resort hotels of the Canadian Rockies and connecting passengers with the overseas service of CP steamships. The Soo played a leading role for 60 years in developing interest in Canada as a tourism destination, resulting in a healthy profit margin for Canadian Pacific, the parent company.

As in his two previous books, Terry uses historical photographs, terminals, maps, locomotives, period advertising, the Rockies, train timetables, exterior and interior views of railway cars, and Pullmans.

Terry's three books would be a great addition to anybody's library. He writes enthusiastically, has excellent knowledge of his subject, and has a sense of history and humour. What could be better?

❧ PREFACE ❧

THE SOO LINE'S FAMOUS TRAINS TO CANADA is a brief history of a small and unique Class 1 railway and its famous international passenger trains. Initially chartered in 1883 to serve the needs of local millers in Minneapolis, the Soo would offer an alternative shipping route to the ports of the eastern seaboard. Bypassing Chicago would eliminate the usurious freight rates established by Chicago-based railways. The new railway would join the Canadian Pacific line at Sault Ste. Marie, Ontario, to Montreal on Canadian Pacific, then into the US on the Boston and Lowell, a Canadian Pacific partner. The new route provided services to Boston and New York ports. A group of Minneapolis-based entrepreneurs, including Charles Pillsbury of C.A. Pillsbury and Company, and W.A. Washburn of Minneapolis Mills and a prominent Minnesota politician, came together and funded the railway construction.

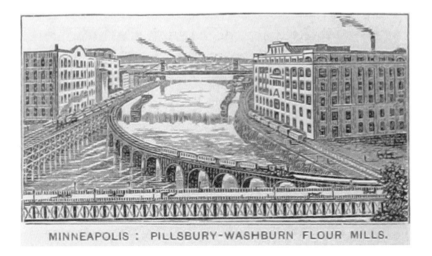

MINNEAPOLIS : PILLSBURY-WASHBURN FLOUR MILLS.

Courtesy Alamy Limited, 6–8 West Central, 127 Olympic Avenue, Milton Park, Abingdon, UK.

But it also tells the story of how Canadian Pacific assumed controlling interest in the Soo Line in the late 1880s. The Soo Line was a considerable gamble for CP that paid off in spades, providing entry into the lucrative US market and levelling the playing field for the CPR to face the onslaught of ferocious competition from James J. Hill, the infamous American railway baron. The "little railway that could" grew to attain giant-killer status, launching famous passenger trains from Chicago, Minneapolis, and St. Paul, meeting head-on the western expansion of the Great Northern Railway and viable, competitive trains to the Atlantic seaboard. Over the years, the Soo Line introduced thousands of Americans to Montreal and Quebec City, the famous Canadian Rockies resorts, and Vancouver, the home port for CP's Pacific steamship services. It successfully competed on the Spokane and Portland routes from Minneapolis to the Pacific Northwest. The year 1923 saw the launch of the Soo Mountaineer, which became North America's most famous and longest two-nation train journey.

The history of the Soo Line's importance to the CPR is relatively undocumented. The "Soo" has always been a solid contributor to the bottom line; today, the revenues for the smallest Class A railway remain exceptional. But what is not common knowledge is the Soo Line's leading role in the first 60 years of the 20th century in developing American interest in Canada as a tourism destination. I worked summer jobs for Canadian Pacific in Banff for ten years during that era, and this book is my contribution to that story.

&ero; ACKNOWLEDGEMENTS &ero;

WHILE SEARCHING FOR INFORMATION about the Soo-Spokane Train Deluxe for my second book, *When Trains Ruled the Kootenays*, I became acquainted with Emory Lubke, archivist with the Soo Line Historical and Technical Society. Emory provided me with a flood of information, digging out historical facts, perspectives, Soo Line photographs, and public timetables. This wealth of information was the spark that ignited my interest to embark on the journey to book number three. Emory, I cannot thank you and your team enough; this book could never have happened without your assistance. I am deeply indebted.

My daughter has been my best cheerleader through three books over the last six years. Chantal, I am so thankful for your support and encouragement in my "second career." I'm sure there have been times when my "trains" obsession drove you nuts, but you never winced!

Readers may note an overlap with my first two books, *When Trains Ruled the Rockies* and *When Trains Ruled the Kootenays*. Indeed there is. My most discerning publisher, Don Gorman, asked me if this book was perhaps the completion of a trilogy about passenger trains in Canada. So, in hindsight, I wish I had thought that far ahead. Thanks, Don. It is obvious why you are the publisher and I'm the student.

I returned to the Whyte Museum of the Canadian Rockies for more information about the 1950s and '60s in Banff, Alberta, particularly the Mountaineer. Once again, Elizabeth Kundert-Cameron, head of archives and special collections, was there to guide me through the numerous avenues of search and research. And when I proposed a book launch at the Whyte Museum, Mollie Riley, programs and events coordinator, went beyond the call of duty, immediately confirming and organizing the event. Thank you, Elizabeth and Mollie, for your faith in me and for assisting me through my publications.

Once again, Chantal Guérin, archival technician at Exporail, the Canadian Railway Museum in Montreal, came to my rescue when I was floundering in my search for early information on the Soo Line and the CPR. Chantal found the information I required and came up with additional 1920s brochure information on the Mountaineer. Chantal, my sincere thanks.

Without the team's support at Rocky Mountain Books, I wouldn't be writing acknowledgements, because there would be no book. Don, Grace, and Jillian, many thanks for your patience and guidance. What an opportunity you've provided me in my senior years!

❧ INTRODUCTION ❧

IN THE SUMMER OF 1948, I was 6 years old when the Gainer family moved to Banff, Alberta, in the heart of the Canadian Rockies. The CPR appointed my dad, FL (Frank) Gainer, as station agent, and the position included a residence on the top floor of the train station. We had a huge balcony overlooking the platform, and I spent hours watching the passengers step off the sleeping cars that stopped directly below. I had lots of choices; there were eight transcontinental trains daily. Thus began my lifelong love affair with passenger trains.

Over the next few years, I savoured every detail of every train. I realized every passenger train had a unique identity, catering to specific customer requirements. Even the physical makeup of the train consist (pronounced *con*-sist) differed. Trains 1 and 2, called the "stop everywhere" trains, the Dominion and the Canadian (introduced in 1955), were visually identifiable, and the passengers carried were as distinct as the trains. And then there was "my" train, the Soo-Mountaineer. It captured me from the start. The physical makeup of the Mountaineer was unmistakable, but it also had intrigue. The Mountaineer operated over North America's longest international train route, bringing thousands of American visitors to Canada every year since its introduction in 1923.

The Mountaineer was only the beginning of my fascination with the Soo Line. In the last few years, I've immersed myself in the Soo Line's mystique and incredible achievements. The "little railway that could" often did! The Soo Line was a niche railway built to serve the agricultural industry. Soo Line management soon spotted another niche opportunity, becoming an early leader in promoting passenger service from the United States to Canada's east and west coasts, feeding the famous Canadian Rockies resorts and connecting with the overseas services of

Canadian Pacific steamships. Famous trains, including the Montreal-Boston Express, the Soo Pacific, the Soo-Spokane-Portland Train Deluxe, the Winnipeger, and the Mountaineer, are the stuff of legends. This perceived gap in the history of North American railways is the backbone of my story.

★ ★ ★

A BRIEF HISTORY
OF THE SOO LINE

Part 1 of this book introduces the upper Midwest
and what would become the cities of Minneapolis
and Saint Paul (abbreviated St. Paul). As settlers
moved west, new industries were established
around the power source provided by the waterfalls
on the Mississippi River. First came the lumber
mills, followed by the "Millers of Minneapolis."
The Soo Line was born out of economic necessity
to transport agricultural goods to the ports of the
eastern seaboard and serve a hungry European
market. Over the years, the Soo Line would exploit a
new and booming tourism market seeking adventure
in Canada.

CHAPTER 1

In the Beginning

The last great ice age ended about twelve thousand years ago. Torrents of glacial meltwater poured down from the north, flooding through the Minnesota Valley, carving out a wide river canyon and waterfall on the Mississippi River below present-day St. Paul. At the height of the glacial melt, the falls were two miles wide and over two hundred feet in height. Over time, the pounding of the water has slowly eroded the falls upstream to their present location at the northeastern edge of today's downtown Minneapolis. The Dakotas had named the waterfalls "Owámniyomni," meaning "Three Whirlpools," the only natural waterfall on the Mississippi.[1]

THE DAKOTA CALLED THE MISSISSIPPI Haha Wakpa, the river of the falls. Oral tradition suggests that the Dakota camped, hunted, and fished in the area, and that the site was sacred. For centuries, the Mississippi had served as a major highway for the Dakota, Ojibwe, and more ancient Indigenous Peoples. Europeans first saw the falls in 1680, when the Dakota guided a wandering Catholic friar from Belgium, Louis Hennepin, to the area. As Europeans were wont to do, he renamed the site Saint Anthony Falls, after his patron saint, St. Anthony of Padua, Spain. Many artists, including the famous German-American painter Albert Bierstadt, have memorialized the falls.

In 1825, the US Army established Fort Snelling as a western outpost. Settlers were to follow and establish small mills to process their grains. In 1849, the town of St. Anthony arose, and Minneapolis followed in 1867.

---

1 "Saint Anthony Falls," Wikipedia, https://en.wikipedia.org/wiki/Saint_Anthony_Falls.

Albert Bierstadt's *The Falls of St. Anthony.* Courtesy commons.wikimedi.org/wiki/commons: Reuse_of_PD-Art-photographs.

Initially, both villages were milling towns but also experienced the boom of the logging industry. Seemingly dedicated to chopping down every tree in Minnesota, the logging companies used the falls to power the many sawmills on the east and west shores. But as the logging petered out and moved further west and north, milling took precedence, and the region prospered.

Minneapolis millers led the country in applying new technologies to the problem of producing fine flour from the hard spring wheat grown on the northern plains. They achieved premium quality by using a series of steel rollers instead of millstones, removing bran fragments with middling purifiers. Since the 1880s, Minneapolis has enjoyed the title of Flour and Milling Capital of the World. But to serve the milling industry, a railway was necessary to transport the flour and milled grains to larger markets on the eastern seaboard and overseas.

CHAPTER 2

The Birth of a Railway

BY 1871, the predecessors of the Milwaukee Road had linked the Twin Cities with Chicago, followed soon after by the Chicago & North Western and the Chicago, Burlington and Quincy (CB & Q). But therein lay the quandary. For the milling industry in Minneapolis to succeed, its products had to reach the eastern seaboard ports for shipment across the Atlantic to Europe. As author Patrick Dorin notes in his book *The Soo Line*, all railroads were Chicago-based, and, as the sole gateway to the east coast, Chicago could (and did) charge usurious freight rates.

The Millers of Minneapolis chose to band together to overcome their dilemma, creating a consortium to build their own railway. William Washburn and Charles Alfred Pillsbury (of Pillsbury fame) led the consortium, and the Minneapolis, Sault Ste. Marie & Atlantic Railway (MSStM&A) received its charter in 1883. The "Millers" owned 75% of the company, and their approach was to bypass Chicago, reaching the east coast through southern Canada to Montreal and then to Boston for trans-Atlantic shipment. From the beginning, the MSStM&A was well funded, and construction soon began to Sault Ste. Marie in northern Michigan to connect with the Canadian Pacific Railway. The railhead reached Sault Ste. Marie on December 10, 1887. In late 1888, the CPR completed a branch line from its mainline at Sudbury to Sault Ste. Marie and the MSStM&A incorporated the Minneapolis & St. Croix Railway, completing dedicated trackage to the Twin Cities.[1]

1 Adam Burns, "Soo Line Railroad (Minneapolis, St. Paul & Sault Ste. Marie)," American-Rails, https://www.american-rails.com/soo.html.

General Mills Flour Mill, Minneapolis, MN, 1954. Courtesy Alamy Limited, 6–8 West Central, 127 Olympic Avenue, Milton Park, Abingdon, UK.

The railway was in business.

West of Minneapolis, construction continued into the rich agricultural country of western Minnesota and the Dakota Territory to ensure a continual supply of the superior spring wheat that produced high-quality flour. In 1887, the consortium's Minneapolis & Pacific Railway reached Boynton and Bismarck. But rapid expansion stretched the parent company's resources, and the Minneapolis, Sault Ste. Marie & Atlantic fell into financial difficulty.

Canadian Pacific realized the link with the MSStM&A was one of its most important connections, providing access to the lucrative American markets. The MSStM&A could easily fall into unfriendly hands, such as the Vanderbilts, who owned the New York Central, or even James J. Hill of the Great Northern. Canadian Pacific's relationship with Hill slowly deteriorated after he pulled out of the CP Syndicate in 1883. It would be in the CPR's interest to shore up the finances of its US partner. Unfortunately, Canadian Pacific had financial difficulties, struggling to pay off debts from completing the transcontinental mainline to Vancouver.

In the end, George Stephen, President of the Canadian Pacific and Donald Smith, a Director and principal investor, used their own money to acquire the properties of the MSStM&A. Both had risked a considerable amount of their fortunes to secure Canadian Pacific's US presence.

In June 1888, Stephen and Smith merged all three railways (Minneapolis & Pacific, Minneapolis & St. Croix, and Minneapolis, Sault Ste. Marie & Atlantic) into a new company, the Minneapolis, St. Paul & Sault Ste. Marie Railway. From its early years, the new railway was known simply as the "Soo Line," the phonetic spelling of Sault, a French word meaning waterfall or rapids. In June 1889, the first passenger train bound for St. Paul left Boston, Massachusetts.[2]

By 1890, Canadian Pacific's increasingly favourable financial position allowed the company to assume all Soo Line debt, replacing Stephen and Smith as majority shareholders. The purchase was one of CPR's best decisions ever made, and the Soo Line began to attract attention.

....
2 Burns.

CHAPTER 3

What a Tangled Web We Weave

THE RELATIONSHIP between George Stephen, Donald Smith, and William Cornelius Van Horne of the Canadian Pacific and James J. Hill of the Great Northern was a convoluted, twisted narrative almost impossible to follow or comprehend. At first, this quartet of railway entrepreneurs and financiers appeared to be a match made in heaven.

Donald Smith and James J. Hill first met in Minneapolis in 1869. At the time, Donald Smith was the chief factor for the Hudson's Bay Company in Canada. He was in St. Paul to meet and negotiate with Metis leader Louis Riel on behalf of the Canadian government. Riel had self-exiled in the United States, fearing for his life if he returned to Canada. Smith also met with Hill, who, among his many business interests, sold supplies to the Free Fur Traders in the Red River Colony, now Manitoba, and the Hudson's Bay Company. The two businessmen were troubled by the Red River uprising.

> The Red River Resistance (also known as the Red River Rebellion) was an uprising in 1869–70 in the Red River Colony. A colony of farmers and hunters, many of them Métis, occupied a corner of Rupert's Land and feared for their culture and land rights under Canadian control. The Métis mounted a resistance and declared a provisional government, hoping to negotiate conditions for entry to Confederation. The uprising led to the creation of the province of Manitoba and the emergence of Métis leader Louis Riel. Riel was a hero to his people, but an outlaw in the eyes of the Canadian government.[1]

1 J.M. Bumsted, "Red River Resistance," *The Canadian Encyclopedia*, https://www.thecanadianencyclopedia.ca/en/article/red-river-rebellion.

In 1870, the trade route between St. Paul and Fort Garry was threatened as the Red River unrest continued. Joseph Howe, Canada's secretary of state for the provinces, was aware of Hill's business reputation and Canadian connections and asked him to travel north to Fort Garry to gather information and report to Ottawa. No one had a grasp of what was transpiring in the colony.

Hill accepted, quickly departing St. Paul even though it was mid-winter. On the stretch from Pembina to Fort Garry, Hill travelled by dogsled. Caught up in a blinding snowstorm, he luckily stumbled on a southbound party led by Donald Smith; otherwise, the harsh prairie winter may have hastened Hill's demise. Smith was quitting Fort Garry, making his way to Ottawa to report to the government. Smith told Hill he'd recommend sending troops to put down the rebellion to the prime minister.

Hill continued to Fort Garry, where he met in person with Riel. But as Riel explained, solving the many issues would take more than a show of strength. One key to the situation was the avoidance of clashes between the numerous tribes. Hill quoted Riel saying, "The tribes could go to war with each other if the white men did not settle their differences soon. The settlers are feeling threatened." The day Hill returned to St. Paul, he telegraphed Howe in Ottawa the essentials of the conflict, followed by a long letter emphasizing Hill's version of the Indian problem.[2]

As history records, Ottawa sent the troops, stabilizing the situation. Through their mutual interests, both commercial and political, Hill and Smith became fast friends, a relationship that would stand fast through many challenges.

Hill understood that a peaceful settlement would encourage immigration to the Canadian West, and Fort Garry (to become Winnipeg) would be the commercial hub. In 1870, Hill and partner Norman Kittson invested with steamboat captain Alexander Griggs and formed the Red River

----

2 Research information from Stephen Sadis, producer and director, *The Empire Builder: James J. Hill and the Great Northern Railway*, documentary (Seattle: Great Northern Filmworks, 2022).

Transportation Company, deploying seven steamboats on the Red and Assiniboine rivers. The company was ultimately successful, serving the new province called Manitoba. In 1873, Donald Smith revisited St. Paul, accompanied by his cousin, George Stephen, the president of the Bank of Montreal. They discussed with Hill and Kittson a proposal to acquire the St. Paul and Pacific Railway, which was in receivership. The St. Paul partners had insufficient funds to finance the venture and relied on Stephen's Bank of Montreal and his New York banking connections to secure the transaction. On May 23, 1879, a new company, St. Paul, Minneapolis and Manitoba Railway, began operations, with George Stephen as president, Kittson as vice president, and Hill as general manager. The railway rewarded its promoters generously, providing the capital and connections for a more ambitious venture, the Canadian Pacific Railway. In 1882, Hill assumed the presidency of St. Paul, Minneapolis and Manitoba, as George Stephen and Donald Smith focused on the Canadian Pacific Syndicate to build Canada's transcontinental railway.

In 1880, Hill agreed to join the syndicate with the specific duties of overseeing construction, although he had reservations about the railway's success. Too busy to supervise the project himself, he recruited William Cornelius Van Horne as general manager. Hill assured Stephen and the CP Syndicate that Van Horne was the most knowledgeable general manager in the railway business, as he eventually proved to be. But the "match made in heaven" soon began to unravel. Hill had always insisted the planned all-Canadian route across the northern shore of Lake Superior was a huge mistake, with no population or industry along the right of way to provide shipping or passenger revenues. He insisted the route should dip into the US at Sault Ste. Marie to Duluth to Minneapolis. From Minneapolis, his railway would be the connector to Winnipeg and the western line of the CPR. (Of course, any vested interest would be purely coincidental.)

Hill never seemed to grasp that Sir John A. Macdonald, the prime minister of Canada, and his government was the CPR Syndicate's client and biggest supporter, insisting on an all-Canadian line. He was particularly incensed that Van Horne, his protégé, dared to support the all-Canadian route against his wishes. In 1883, Hill pulled out of the syndicate, accusing the CPR of wrongdoing, including the misuse of St. Paul, Minneapolis and

Manitoba Railway funds. Some of his complaints were legitimate, and he vowed revenge. Hill announced he would extend his railway, renamed the Great Northern, to the Pacific coast and, by 1893, reached Puget Sound and Seattle. Thus began a bitter, 30-year battle with Canadian Pacific in North Dakota, Manitoba, the Pacific Northwest, and southern British Columbia.

But Hill's departure from the CP Syndicate and consequent actions were bizarre. His publicly expressed resentment and hostility were directed only at the company entity and personally at Van Horne. Donald Smith and George Stephen escaped his wrath, despite their top executive positions with the CPR. Even more convoluted were Smith and Stephen's continued loyalty to Hill. Both continued to hold influential positions in Great Northern, far more extensive than their CPR holdings. After the reorganization of Great Northern in 1901, when Hill finally seized control of rival Northern Pacific, Smith surfaced as the third-largest shareholder in the new company called Northern Securities Limited, the holding company for the Great Northern, Northern Pacific, and Chicago, Burlington and Quincy. Similarly, George Stephens's holdings and wealth lay in his Great Northern investments, not the CPR he led for so many years. Strange twists, indeed.

When Smith and Stephen came to the rescue of the Soo Line in 1888, at considerable risk to their personal wealth, they suspected Hill would eventually take over their position. But he had no interest, viewing the Soo Line as a duplication of his railway and, as a result, redundant. It was an unusual miscalculation by the wily railway baron. The purchase of the Soo Line assets in 1890 by the CPR provided unfettered access to Midwest markets, setting up shop in Hill's hometown.

CHAPTER 4

Westward Ho through Great Northern's Backyard

BEFORE COMPLETING the Great Northern mainline to Seattle in 1893, Hill and CP interlined traffic between the Twin Cities and the Pacific Port of Vancouver. But that would change when Hill's line opened. Canadian Pacific wanted to protect this traffic and financed a Soo Line extension to Portal, North Dakota, on the Saskatchewan border. Construction was completed in 1893 and joined by a CP connection to the mainline at Moose Jaw, Saskatchewan. The third Soo rail line to Canada was completed in 1904 to Winnipeg, crossing the international boundary at Noyes, Minnesota, and Emerson, Manitoba. Canadian Pacific's access to the Twin Cities, Dakotas, and the Midwest was secured.

With the three gateways now connected to CPR lines in Canada, the Soo Line proceeded with plans to extend access to the rich farmlands of North Dakota and the Red River Valley. The activity, noted by officials of the Great Northern, set off alarm bells inside the company headquarters.

James Hill received the news while vacationing on his yacht. In response to his son Louis Hill's request, he agreed that the Great Northern would start a competing survey to head off the threat and that Hill would go to Montreal to initiate talks with Thomas Shaughnessy, President of the CPR. But Shaughnessy instead travelled to Minneapolis to meet with his Soo Line counterpart, Vice President and General Manager Edmund Pennington. Hill then arranged a meeting with Shaughnessy and Pennington, hoping to strengthen his hand by inviting Darius Miller,

Bowbells, ND, postcard of grain elevators constructed c. 1905, Soo westward expansion. Photographer unknown. Courtesy Soo Line Historical and Technical Society Archives Collection.

President of the Chicago, Burlington and Quincy Railway, to sit at the negotiating table. Louis Hill ordered the construction crews to begin grading the newly surveyed line the day before the meeting to prove the Great Northern's intent.[1]

The bluff and intimidation did not work. Hill and Miller realized Shaughnessy and Pennington were not easily discouraged. The Soo Line was undaunted, proceeding with surveys and constructing a line across the northern part of North Dakota. Great Northern would have to follow suit, building new lines to protect its territory. As reported in the *Grand Forks Herald*, thus began North Dakota's Railway War of 1905. The Soo would announce a new line, and Great Northern would counter and build nearby.

....

1   John C. Hudson, *North Dakota's Railway War of 1905* (Minneapolis: University of Minnesota Printing Services, 1981), 6.

Soo Line elevators, Flaxton, ND, c. 1910. Photographer unknown. Courtesy Soo Line Historical and Technical Society Archives Collection.

Leases along railway side tracks were made to grain elevators, lumber companies and coal dealers. The Soo granted 29 elevator leases early in 1905 to the Atlantic Elevator Company of Minneapolis to construct a 50,000-bushel elevator in every town along the new line. By November 1905, 100 new elevators were completed or under construction on the Soo Lines. More than fifty new towns were established along the Soo and Great Northern lines as the companies battled to secure territory.[2]

The war would last over a year and change the state's settlement. There was no clear-cut winner in the battle for dominance in North Dakota; if someone kept score, it would appear to be a draw. But it did establish the Soo Line as a formidable competitor for other railways of the upper Midwest. Great Northern would not "have its way" with the Soo. But the end of hostilities in North Dakota did not end the struggle. For the next decade, the Soo, CPR, and Great Northern continued to fight for supremacy from North Dakota to the Canadian West.

2 Hudson, 15–16.

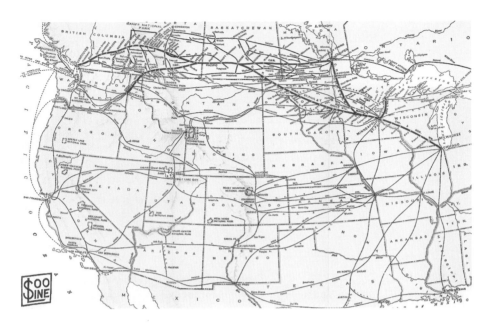

The Soo Line, c. 1910. Courtesy Soo Line Historical and Technical Society Archives Collection.

Enderlin, ND, depot and elevator. Courtesy Soo Line Historical and Technical Society Archives Collection.

In 1905, a fourth player entered the "game" in Washington state and Idaho. Daniel Corbin, an old foe of both the CPR and James J. Hill, suddenly became the CPR and the Soo Line's best ally in the struggle with Hill and the Great Northern for supremacy in southeastern British Columbia. Gold discoveries in Rossland and rich silver, lead, and zinc deposits throughout the West Kootenays spurred frantic railway construction in the 1890s. In Crowsnest Pass of the East Kootenays, rich deposits of industrial-grade coal were discovered, leading to another frenzy of railway activity. Corbin planned to develop his claim on Coal Mountain and envisioned a rail connection from Spokane, Washington, to the Canadian border, connecting with the CPR's Crowsnest Pass route.

Corbin built the first railway from the US into the Kootenays in 1893, the Nelson & Fort Sheppard Railway, the Canadian continuation of his Spokane Falls & Northern Railway from Spokane, successfully challenging the CPR in the West Kootenay. But in 1897, a mysterious buyer, operating many false fronts, wrestled away control of his railways. The mysterious buyer turned out to be none other than James J. Hill. Although Corbin made a fortune on the takeover, he never forgave Hill for "stealing" his railroads. Hill's successful takeover gave him complete control over Spokane and the Inland Empire of Eastern Washington. Through the 1920s, Spokane was the financial heart of the mining and smelting industry in Idaho, Montana, and British Columbia.

Corbin saw the opportunity to build a rail line, the Spokane International, from Spokane to the Canadian border, as the first step to breaking Hill's monopoly in the Pacific Northwest and Corbin's first step in gaining a measure of revenge. Corbin approached Thomas Shaughnessy, president of the CPR, with his plan, as he lacked the sufficient financial backing to complete the line. Old foes became allies, united against a common enemy. The age-old saying, "the enemy of my enemy is my friend," comes to mind. The CPR agreed to underwrite the bonds, becoming the majority partner. In 1906, Spokane International reached the border, connected to the CPR Crowsnest line by an eight-mile spur to the village of Yahk, BC. Corbin then developed his Crowsnest mines, transporting the coal to the lucrative US market via Spokane International in direct competition with

Hill and the Great Northern Collieries, located a scant few miles away. The completion of Spokane International was a positive development for the increasingly aggressive expansion of the Soo Line passenger service, as detailed in Part 2 of this book.

Soo Line cars loading at flour mill, Minneapolis, MN, c. 1910. Photographer unknown. Courtesy Soo Line Historical and Technical Society Archives Collection.

CHAPTER 5

Wisconsin Central, the Final Piece of the Puzzle

THE EVOLUTION OF THE WISCONSIN CENTRAL differed dramatically from the Soo Line. The birth of the Soo, initially financed by the Minneapolis milling industry, was in stark contrast to the beginnings of the Wisconsin Central. Although the original promoters were Wisconsin residents, they needed more financial backing to build a line from Chicago and Milwaukee to the shores of Lake Superior through central Wisconsin. The Federal Land Grant program would not be sufficient to generate enough revenue for construction, and the search for capital led to Gardner Colby, a Boston banker. "Beware of bankers bearing gifts" might have been appropriate advice for the original promoters, led by Judge George Reed, his brother Curtis Reed, and Matt Wadleigh.

Initially, Colby found Judge Reed's knowledge and connections in Wisconsin's political world valuable in laying the groundwork for the railroad and sorting problematic issues. But by 1871, when Reed's influence was no longer necessary, he and his partners were shunted to the sidelines and forced out of the company. Colby chose Elijah Phillips as the chief construction engineer and created a construction company to build the railroad. Phillips's incompetence and their combined greed proved to be a disaster. But it was an age-old formula in the early history of American railroads. Feed the construction company, rape the railroad, and declare bankruptcy to avoid paying bills.

It took until 1877 to complete the route to Lake Superior. In 1878, Gardner Colby's son Charles became president, somehow surviving the graft and corruption of the previous management. But by 1879, the railroad

Wisconsin Central locomotive, c. 1890. Location and photographer unknown.
Courtesy Soo Line Historical and Technical Society Archives Collection.

was bankrupt, and the trustees took over the line. Charles Colby remained as president, but the trustees wielded power.

The trustees and the board of directors authorized the push to St. Paul and Minneapolis, and by 1880 the Wisconsin Central reached Chippewa Falls and Eau Claire in its namesake state. An agreement with the Omaha Railroad provided trackage rights for the few remaining miles to the Twin Cities. In February 1886, the Wisconsin Central reached Chicago. The future looked bright, but the financial collapse of 1893 put many railways into receivership, including the Wisconsin Central. Henry Whitcomb and Howard Morris were appointed receivers. By 1898, the US economy was back on track, and the company planned to emerge from bankruptcy protection.

On July 13, 1899, the Wisconsin Central Railway (a new and separately chartered company) purchased the entire system at a foreclosure sale. Henry Whitcomb had proved himself to be a skillful manager and became general manager and president of the new Wisconsin Central.

Upon his appointment, Whitcomb acted immediately, upgrading all company-owned terminals. He negotiated new, long-term contracts for leased and rental properties with better terms. The Great Northern Railway granted Whitcomb permanent access to trackage rights between St. Paul and Minneapolis, and he purchased land on Boom Island, developing the Twin City terminal. Successful negotiations with the Illinois Central Railway garnered land for a downtown terminal in Chicago. The last major construction project of the Wisconsin Central began under Whitcomb's presidency, the 163-mile line to Duluth. President Whitcomb retired in 1906, but new president William Bradford continued construction, reaching Superior, Wisconsin, in 1909. Passenger service began to Duluth from Chicago the following year. A new depot, constructed near the lakefront, was the most elegant the Wisconsin Central ever owned.[1]

But a funny thing happened on the way to solvency. Canadian Pacific had long recognized that an increased US presence was crucial to future success. Throughout 1908, CP and the Soo Line stealthily purchased over 50 per cent of Wisconsin Central Railway stock. The Soo Line assumed control of the board of directors, forging a 99-year lease agreement and assigned operations of the Wisconsin Central to its Chicago division. Canadian Pacific's "secret weapon" skillfully orchestrated the takeover, and the Soo Line became a serious player in the Midwest.

The last westward expansion for the Soo commenced in 1905, grading and laying rails from Flaxton to Crosby, North Dakota, accessing new wheat-growing territories. Slowly, the line extended west and, by 1913, reached Whitetail, Montana, seven miles south of the Canadian border. Glacier National Park was planned as the final Montana destination, with a possible link-up to the CPR in southern Alberta. But when World War I broke out, that plan was permanently scrapped. Whitetail would remain the Soo's westernmost extension.

1 John A. Gjevre, *Saga of the Soo: East, West and to the North*, vol. 3 (Moorhead, MN: Agassiz Publications, 2006), 54.

Whitetail, MT, 1977. The last stop for the Soo Line in the western United States. Photographer Tom Carlson. Courtesy Soo Line Historical and Technical Society Archives Collection.

Soo depot and grain elevators, Dooley, MT. Third-last stop before Whitetail, c. 1914. Photographer unknown. Courtesy Soo Line Historical and Technical Society Archives Collection.

Soo's Duluth, MN, depot, exterior and interior. Photographer unknown.
Courtesy Archives of the Lake Superior Railroad Museum.

Soo Line depot, Duluth, MN, with trains, 1935. Photographer unknown. Courtesy Soo Line Historical and Technical Society Archives Collection.

In one of the last bursts of construction, "Soo rails reached Duluth-superior in 1909 from Onamia on the Brooten line, and the following year the Plummer line reached Moose Lake. Fortuitously, in 1909, the leased *Wisconsin Central* had already reached Superior from the south. The newly-leased railway was finishing a magnificent depot in Duluth and became the Soo's finest and largest depot."[2] The Soo became a formidable player in the Upper Midwest.

2 John A. Gjevre, *Three Generations West: Saga of the Soo*, vol. 2 (Moorhead, MN: Agassiz Publications, 1995), 54.

CHAPTER 6

Setting the Stage
Canadian Pacific Steamship Company and Canadian Pacific Hotels and Resorts

WILLIAM CORNELIUS VAN HORNE was a true visionary. He recognized that his transcontinental railway had far more potential than transporting goods and raw materials. There was now a direct link between Europe and Asia, eliminating weeks of sailing halfway around the globe. It was labelled the "All-Red Route," providing the fastest access to the furthest reaches of the British Empire. But Van Horne was not content just being a land link. In 1887, he began trans-Pacific service from Vancouver to Asia.

The purchase of the SS *Abyssinia*, SS *Parthia*, and the SS *Batavia* from Cunard was the initial step to create a fleet of luxury ocean liners built to CPR specifications. The CPR named the new division the Canadian Pacific Steamship Company. By 1891, the all-new Empress class ocean liners transported mail, silk, tea and passengers to and from Asia, dominating first-class trans-Pacific travel with three of the most opulent liners in the world; the *Empress of India*, the *Empress of China*, the *Empress of Japan*.[1]

Van Horne stepped down as president of the CPR in 1899, but remained chairman of the board until 1910. His successor, Thomas Shaughnessy, supported his vision that CP would span the world. In 1903, the company began trans-Atlantic service, initially between Halifax, Nova Scotia, and

....

1 Chung Library, http://chung.library.ubc.ca/collection-themes/canadian-pacific-railway/travel-and-tourism-c-p-r.

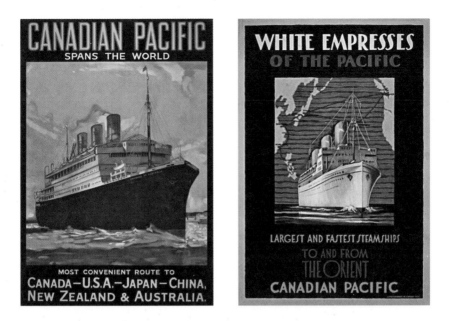

Canadian Pacific steamships poster images, c. 1910. Courtesy Terry Gainer collection.

the United Kingdom, and a shipbuilding frenzy followed. In 1906, CP launched the sister ships the *Empress of Britain* and the *Empress of Ireland*. The *Empress of Asia* and its sister ship, *Empress of Russia*, entered the Pacific service in 1913, followed by the *Empress of Canada* in 1922. Canadian Pacific Steamship Company became a dominant international shipping line, globally recognized as a luxury world cruise line.

A legendary figure in the annals of Canadian history as a foremost railway builder, Van Horne is also revered as the pioneer of tourism in Canada. His famous quote, made on the site of the Banff Springs Hotel, "If we cannot export the scenery, we will import the tourists," marked the beginning of his luxury chain of hotels along the route of the Canadian Pacific. In 1886, Glacier House in Rogers Pass and Mount Stephen House in Field, BC, opened to international acclaim, followed by the Banff Springs Hotel in 1888 and the Chateau Lake Louise in 1892. The pieces were in place to dominate the world of tourism, but Van Horne realized the success of these ventures lay in attracting American business and carriage trade traffic. The Soo Line became Van Horne's vehicle to transport America to Canada.

The Banff Springs Hotel, c. 1930. Photographer Byron Harmon. Courtesy Whyte Museum of the Canadian Rockies and Archives, Byron Harmon Fonds, V263/NA-3737.

In 1889, the Soo Line inaugurated its first cross-border passenger service, the Montreal-Boston Express, from the Twin Cities. The first-class service entered Canada at Sault Ste. Marie, travelling to Montreal on the CP line, then to Boston via the Boston and Lowell (to become the Boston & Maine) Railway.

In 1894, on completion of the line to Portal, North Dakota, the Soo commenced passenger service from St. Paul and Minneapolis to Moose Jaw, Banff, Lake Louise, Vancouver, and Seattle, inaugurating the Soo Pacific Express. The train entered Canada at North Portal, Saskatchewan, connecting to the CPR mainline at Moose Jaw, Saskatchewan. At Huntingdon Junction, BC, the train split into two sections, with Seattle through cars joining the awaiting Seattle and International. The balance of the train continued to Vancouver.

In 1906, on completion of the Spokane International line to the Canadian border, CP and the Soo ordered six complete train sets from Barney and Smith. In 1907, the daily service of the Soo-Spokane Train Deluxe began from the Twin Cities to Spokane, Washington, breaking Great Northern's monopoly in the Pacific Northwest. The Soo-Spokane entered Canada at North Portal, Saskatchewan, and travelled through Crowsnest Pass in Alberta and British Columbia before re-entering the United States at Eastport, Idaho, then to Spokane. In 1908, the route was extended to Portland, Oregon, in agreement with Union Pacific and renamed the Soo-Spokane-Portland Train Deluxe.

In the summer of 1923, the Soo-Mountaineer began a 38-year run. With service from Chicago to St. Paul, Minneapolis, Portal, Moose Jaw, Banff, and Vancouver, the Mountaineer became the Soo Line's flagship and most lucrative route.

The longest-running Soo service from the Twin Cities to Canada was the overnight train to Winnipeg, Manitoba. Initially branded as the Manitoba Express, the service, inaugurated on November 21, 1904, operated until 1967 and provided connections to the mainline trains east to Toronto and Montreal and westbound to the Canadian Rockies and Vancouver.

The Soo Line fed passengers to CP ships sailing from Canada's Atlantic and Pacific ports for over 50 years and transported thousands of tourists yearly to CP's Grand Resorts in the Canadian Rockies. But the traffic was not only one-way. From the 1890s through the 1920s, from Seattle and the Port of Vancouver, the CP-Soo Line trains were the fastest route from Asia, Alaska, and Western Canada to Minneapolis, St. Paul, and Chicago. The trains were innovative and revered, and the dining cars were famous for outstanding food. There was good reason for Soo's tag line, "The Best Meals on Wheels."

Brochure courtesy Soo Line Historical and Technical Society Archives Collection.

FAMOUS TRAINS
OF THE SOO

The second part of this book features the famous
passenger trains to Canada operated by the Soo Line
from 1883 through 1967. The 1912 brochure details
the far-flung passenger empire.

The "Famous Trains to Canada" originated
in St. Paul, Minneapolis, or Chicago, but not all
travellers hailed from the larger centres. The Soo
Line had passenger trains that criss-crossed the
upper Midwest, serving towns and small cities. The
slick marketing campaigns championed Canada as
a favoured destination, targeting rural Wisconsin,
Minnesota, and North Dakota, as well as urban
promotions. Supported by the Soo Line network
of depots and station agents, affordable tours to
the Canadian Rockies were readily available. The
summer tour trains offered a curious mix of rural
and urban travellers.

For a small Class 1 railway, the Soo Line punched well above its weight. Despite fierce competition from Great Northern and Northern Pacific, Soo passenger trains were popular and competitive. Into the 1950s, daily trains conveniently connected rural travellers to the famous trains to Canada. Minneapolis, St. Paul, and Chicago hubs collected the most transferring passengers. Still, slick connections to the long-distance trains were possible at many divisional points, avoiding the hubbub of the big city, as per the following timetable.

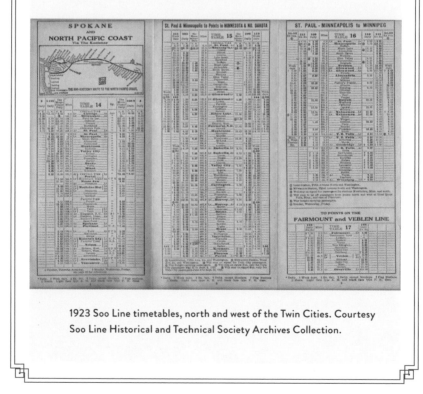

1923 Soo Line timetables, north and west of the Twin Cities. Courtesy Soo Line Historical and Technical Society Archives Collection.

A sample of the small cities served by the Soo, west of the Twin Cities, included Pollock, South Dakota; Bismarck, Hankinson, Enderlin, Drake, and Minot, North Dakota; and communities as far west as Whitetail, Montana.

Similar Soo Line connections were available from eastern Minnesota, Wisconsin, and points in Illinois, east to Montreal or west to the Canadian Rockies and Vancouver. Duluth, Superior, Milwaukee, Wabasha, Rhinelander, Chippewa Falls, Fond du Lac, and Eau Claire were small cities served by Soo passenger trains east of Minneapolis and St. Paul.

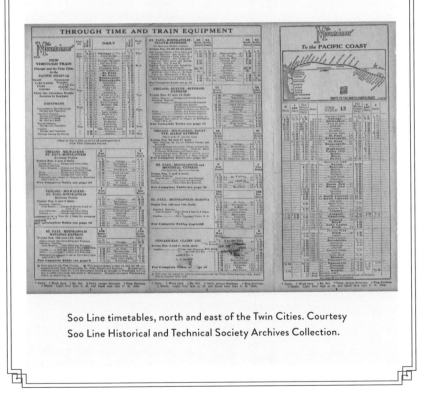

Soo Line timetables, north and east of the Twin Cities. Courtesy Soo Line Historical and Technical Society Archives Collection.

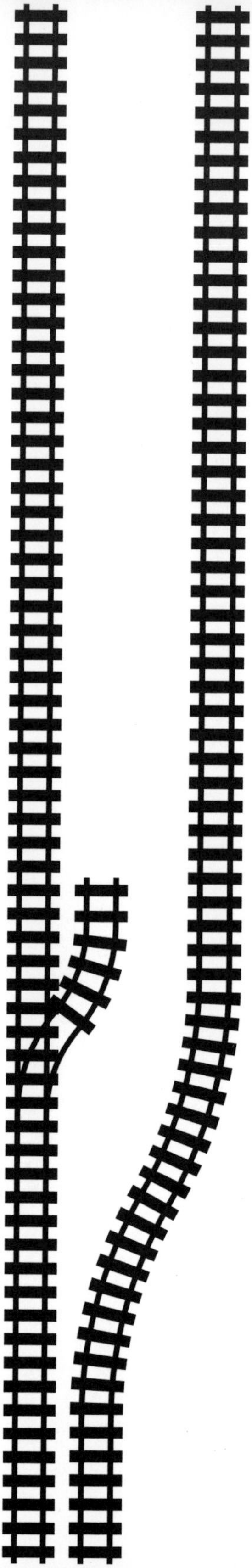

CHAPTER 7

The Atlantic Limited

ON JUNE 3, 1889, the inaugural Montreal-Boston Express steamed from Minneapolis and St. Paul for the two-night journey to Boston. Simultaneously, the westbound departure from Boston departed on the same day. The trains were designated #7 westbound and #8 eastbound. The participating railways, Canadian Pacific, the Soo Line, and Boston and Lowell, agreed to pool their resources to build new rail cars, offering quality service to the eastern seaboard. Each railway purchased equal equipment from car builders Barney and Smith, including elegant wooden sleeping cars featuring the all-new covered vestibules. The service levels were unsurpassed; the dining cars were famous for gleaming mahogany interiors, exquisite food, white linen, and sterling silverware. Each departure included a baggage car, three coaches, a dining car, and two sleeping cars. The Soo sleepers (Minneapolis and Minnesota) were ten sections, with one drawing room.

In 1893, now re-labelled the Atlantic Limited, the train was equal to any passenger service in the US or Canada. The train's immediate success prompted the construction of additional sleepers, adding the slightly longer 12-section and one drawing-room design.

In 1893, the eastbound schedule departed Minneapolis daily at 6:35 p.m. and St. Paul at 7:20. An overnight run through Prentice, Rhinelander, and Gladstone arrived at Sault Ste. Marie and the border at 10:20 in the morning. The train continued east on the CPR line, reaching Sudbury and CP's mainline at 5:55 p.m. The train passed through North Bay, Renfrew, and Ottawa, arriving in Montreal at 9:05 a.m. All cars were through cars, and, after a change of locomotives, #8 departed Montreal at 9:30 a.m., arriving in Newport, Maine, at 1:05 p.m. At this point, the Boston and

The Atlantic Limited, c. 1890. Photographer unknown. Courtesy Soo Line Historical and
Technical Society Archives Collection.

Lowell (to become the Boston & Maine) assumed operation of the train,
passing through Plymouth, Concord, Lowell, and Manchester, arriving
in Boston at 8:50 p.m., completing a two-day, two-night journey. The
westbound departure, train #7 from Boston, departed at 9:30 a.m. and
arrived in Minneapolis two days later at 10:05 a.m.

A second connection to Boston, jointly operated by the CPR and the
Boston and Lowell, left Montreal at 8:00 p.m., arriving in Boston the
following morning at 7:30 a.m. The return departed Boston at 8:30 p.m.,
arriving in Montreal at 8:20 a.m.

Connections were also available from the Twin Cities through Montreal
to New York. The Rutland Railroad's Mount Royal departed Montreal daily
at 7:40 p.m. The train offered all amenities, including dining, sleeping, and
parlour car service. Arrival in New York via Rutland, Troy, and Albany was
at 7:26 a.m. the following day. A second daily service, named the Green
River Flyer, was a day train with a parlour car and dining car, departing
Montreal at 8:50 a.m. and arriving in New York at 8:00 p.m.

Early cover of the Soo Line passenger schedule, Montreal–Boston Express.
Courtesy Soo Line Historical and Technical Society Archives Collection.

The dream of the Atlantic connection from Minneapolis became a reality. The Soo Line's passenger and freight service offered a seamless connection to the ports of Montreal and Boston. The "Millers of Minneapolis" had broken the stranglehold wielded for so long by Chicago-based railways, and the Atlantic Limited opened the door to tourism opportunities in the province of Quebec. The carriage trade of the Midwest now had first-class access to Montreal and the eastern seaboard. Van Horne's American strategy to feed the CP transportation empire was emerging.

Via the "SOO-PACIFIC" LINE the traveler enjoys between Calgary and San Francisco over four days of the grandest Mountain Scenery in the world. Scenery which leaves impressions on the memory never to be effaced by the passage of time, of the glories of three great Mountain Ranges

What to do at Banff	What to do at Laggan	What to do at Field
Visit the hot Sulphur springs. Take the drive around Bow Valley. See the Buffalo herd in the park. Climb some of the numerous nearby peaks	Visit the Lakes in the Clouds. Ride the trail to Saddleback Mountain. Take the trip to the Valley of the Ten Peaks. See the beautiful Paradise Valley	Visit the wonderful Yoho Valley. Stop at the Chalet at Emerald Lake. Take the trail Emerald Lake to Yoho Lake. See the stupendous Takakkaw Falls

THREE SISTERS
10,000 Feet

These tremendous uplifts of stratified rocks of the Davonian and Carboniferous ages guard the entrance to the Rockies. A valley lies at their feet, back of which the mountains raise in solid masses
[Seen from the Train]

MOUNT RUNDLE
10,000 Feet

It rises with up-tilted terraces and sides furrowed and trenched by snowslides. From the valley it appears to have two summits, and so it is sometimes called Twin Peaks
[Seen from the Train]

CASCADE MOUNTAIN
9,796 Feet

Towering majestically and dominating the whole scene at Banff is Cascade Mountain, a huge, time-worn pyramid, ribbed and scarred by avalanche and tempest
[Seen from the Train]

In 1897, Laggan was the station stop for Lake Louise. Initially, the hamlet was called "Holt City" but was renamed Laggan on the arrival of the railway in 1883. In 1914, the station's name changed to Lake Louise. The literature also identifies ticket office locations in Chicago, Cincinnati, and St. Paul. Courtesy Soo Line Historical and Technical Society Archives Collection.

In 1893, the company entered the trans-Atlantic service, cashing in on the thousands of people emigrating from Europe to North America. In 1896, CP added the Empresses of Britain and Ireland to the fleet and introduced its new holiday cruise program to Europe, the Caribbean, and the Mediterranean, capturing the imagination of the adventurous American travel market. The Atlantic Limited was now feeding the ports of Montreal and Quebec City year-round, with first-class tourists from the Twin Cities, Chicago, and Milwaukee.

CHAPTER 8

The Soo Pacific Express

IN 1893, THE SOO EXTENDED THE LINE from Enderlin to the Canadian border at Portal, North Dakota. Canadian Pacific built a branch line from Moose Jaw, Saskatchewan, through Estevan to Portal, completing a west coast connection. The Soo wasted little time inaugurating passenger service. On September 25, 1893, the Soo Pacific Limited departed from St. Paul and Minneapolis for Vancouver and Seattle, the Soo Line's first direct assault on the Great Northern monopoly from the Twin Cities to the Northwest and the Pacific. The Soo Line numbered the westbound departure from St. Paul as train #107 and the eastbound from Seattle and Vancouver as #108.

Leading the train, with engineer J.A. Stinson at the throttle, fireman Henry Gunther, and conductor C.H. Mathews, was engine #40. The consist included a baggage car, second-class coach, first-class coach, a diner, the sleeper Wisconsin, and a tourist sleeper. Departing St. Paul at 9:20 a.m., the three-night journey passed through Minnesota, North Dakota, Saskatchewan, Alberta, British Columbia, and Washington state, arriving in Seattle at 5:25 p.m.

On day one, the Soo Pacific travelled to the international boundary at Portal, North Dakota, where a CPR locomotive took over to the mainline at Moose Jaw, Saskatchewan. On day two, the train joined CP's Pacific Express across the Canadian prairies to Calgary, then into the Rocky Mountains with stops at the CP resorts of Banff Springs Hotel, the Chalet at Lake Louise, Mount Stephen House in Field, BC, and Glacier House at the foot of the Illecillewaet Glacier. It was a downhill run from Glacier to Revelstoke, Kamloops, and Huntingdon Junction (Abbotsford), British Columbia, where the train split on day three. The Seattle through cars

Yoho Valley, Field, B. C.

Yoho Valley, reached from Field, by two splendid trails, is one of the most beautiful in the world. It is a deep valley in the midst of which runs a mighty stream with banks fringed by heavy forests. Here is found a veritable mine of wonders, the mammoth Takakkaw Falls, with a leap of 1,200 feet, Laughing Falls, Twin Falls, the Wapta Glacier and the great Mts. of Gordon and Balfour. In many respects this valley is the greatest ever discovered and is a shrine no mountain lover should miss

The Great Yoho Glacier, near Field, B. C.

From *Soo Pacific Notes*, Yoho Valley and the Great Yoho Glacier. Courtesy Soo Line Historical and Technical Society Archives Collection.

travelled on the Seattle, Lake Shore, and Eastern Railway for the final leg, arriving at 5:25 p.m. Soo passengers bound for Vancouver, Victoria, or sailings to Asia remained on board the Pacific Express, arriving in Vancouver at 1:00 p.m.

Underlying the success of the Soo Pacific was the conviction by the management of the Soo Line and the CPR that a Pacific coast connection through Canada offering seamless travel to Asia, plus the newly introduced Alaska sailings, was intrinsic. The eastern seaboard and the Midwest populations were perfect targets for railways, and urbanization was in full swing. New York's population quadrupled to four million from the Civil

War to 1914, and Chicago exploded from 100,000 to two million. As a result, the consumer base was wealthier, more condensed, and easier to reach.

The 1890s marked the emergence of advertising as an integral component of all successful business activity. In 1883, *Ladies' Home Journal* and *Life Magazine* began publication, followed by other glossy and famous journals, including *Cosmopolitan*, *Munsey's*, *Literary Digest*, and *Vogue*. In 1891, advertising guru Nathan Fowler identified that women made most household purchasing decisions, and companies should reassess their messaging. The marketing aids of the day included newspaper and magazine advertising, plus colourful posters and elaborate brochures targeting travel agencies and booking agents. Canadian Pacific and the Soo Line were savvy marketers and rode the new wave of advertising.

Public spaces, billboards, telegraph offices, and high-traffic railway stations featured full-colour displays. CP and Soo took that to the next level, utilizing colourized photography in sophisticated publications. One such publication was a booklet available to prospective clients called *Soo Pacific Notes*, detailing the three-day journey through the Rockies to Vancouver. Images from the 1897 publication set the standard for advertising well ahead of the times. The booklets, treasured by travellers, were packaged with travel documents and became valuable souvenirs.

The Soo and CP marketing efforts were brilliant. The Banff Springs Hotel, Chateau Lake Louise, Mount Stephen House, and Glacier House became travel industry buzzwords, spurring adventurous travellers to Canada. The summer traffic from Chicago, St. Paul, and Minneapolis boomed, and the Canadian Pacific ships and seamless connections to Asia and Alaska attracted more adventurous long-haul patrons. The Soo Pacific was a success story. Once again, Van Horne's vision of a vertically integrated company paid off in spades.

CHAPTER 9

The Manitoba Express, the Winnipeg Express, the Winnipeger

IN 1904, THE SOO LINE COMPLETED the rail link from Glenwood, North Dakota, to Noyes, Minnesota, connecting to the CPR's Winnipeg line. The Soo now had a third and crucial link to Canada. Freight service began immediately, and passenger service soon followed. On November 21, the first Manitoba Express departed St. Paul and Minneapolis for Winnipeg.

Hill's Great Northern had provided passenger service to Winnipeg since the mid-1880s, and the Soo management realized competition would be tough. Accordingly, it pulled out all the stops.

Edmund Pennington, president of the Soo Line, declared the Manitoba Express "the finest in the Northwest." In 1904, the consist included a mail car, baggage car, two coaches, a dining car, and a first-class sleeper, sleek and newly constructed. The food service was second to none; dinner choices were varied to meet all tastes. Table d'hôte dinner suggestions included soup, salad, and dessert, with broiled lake fish, grilled lamb chops, broiled beefsteak, Spanish omelet, or browned corned beef hash with two eggs. Breakfasts were an egg lover's delight, with fried eggs, boiled eggs, shirred eggs à la creole, and omelets. Bacon and ham, along with broiled fish, were the selected meats. Hash browns or potatoes au gratin rounded out the selection.

In 1909, the name of the train changed to the Winnipeg Express. Winnipeg grew exponentially from the mid-1880s as the Canadian Pacific Railway brought thousands of farmer-immigrants to the prairies. In 1887,

THE NEW WINNIPEG TRAIN

ON THE "SOO LINE."

THE FINEST TRAIN IN THE NORTHWEST.

E. PENNINGTON, 2d Vice-Pres. and Gen'l Mgr.   W. R. CALLAWAY, Gen'l Passenger Agent.

MINNEAPOLIS, MINNESOTA.

Courtesy Soo Line Historical and Technical Society Archives Collection.

the new Winnipeg Grain and Produce Exchange became established in financial circles, and business traffic between Chicago, the Twin Cities, and Winnipeg flourished. Initially a forum for cash trades in Canadian grains, the exchange introduced futures trading in 1904 for wheat, barley, oats, flax, and rye. In 1908, reorganized as the Winnipeg Grain Exchange, it became known as Canada's most important grain and financial futures market.

By 1912, four railroads served Winnipeg, including the Canadian Pacific, Soo Line, Canadian Northern, and Great Northern. The stockyards and freight-handling facilities had given rise to other industries employing large numbers of people and producing fortunes for the local owners.

A Modern Railway

TWIN CITIES TO WINNIPEG, FIFTEEN HOURS.

3/10 of one per cent Grade.
3000 Ties to the Mile.
80-pound Steel Rails.
16-foot Road Bed.
Gravel Ballast.
Modern Passenger Equipment.
Dining Car Service.
Buffet Library Service.
Comfortable Sleeping Cars.

Scenic Through Car Routes
TWIN CITIES—WINNIPEG.
TWIN CITIES—BOSTON.
TWIN CITIES—NORTH PACIFIC.

Courtesy Soo Line Historical and Technical Society Archives Collection.

Slaughterhouses and meatpacking firms were built along a spur line from Arlington to the Winnipeg yards. The largest of these was Gordon, Ironside and Fares, a company that shipped at least 50,000 head of cattle for export every year. In 1906, it processed more animals than any other company in the world.[1] The Soo's re-branding as the Winnipeg Express capitalized on the city's increasing recognition as an important commercial centre.

Over the years, the train became affectionately known by patrons and employees as the Winnipeger. In 1928, recognizing the public's choice, the train was renamed and advertised as the Winnipeger, one of the few passenger trains that continued to operate through World War II.

The early 1950s brought much uncertainty to the Soo Line's passenger system. Still, the Winnipeger and the Mountaineer were the only operating

1 "Manitoba 150 Excerpt #4: Winnipeg 1912," University of Manitoba Press, https://uofmpress.ca/blog/entry/manitoba-150-excerpt-4-winnipeg-1912.

trains that did not suffer debilitating cuts to equipment or service. As late as 1952, the Soo Line continued to improve the Winnipeger. All trains were dieselized from St. Paul through Winnipeg, and equipped with new dining club lounge cars. A typical departure included a mail car, baggage car, two air-conditioned coaches with reclining seats, one Grove sleeper with ten roomettes and four bedrooms, and one refurbished Soo Line sleeper with six sections, five double bedrooms and a dining club lounge. The equipment, continually upgraded, reflected modern sleeping accommodation and dining trends, and the most enduring Soo passenger service boasted sparkling on-time performance. The Winnipeger was the fastest passenger train operated by the Soo Line.

CHAPTER 10

The Soo-Spokane-Portland
Train Deluxe

THOMAS SHAUGHNESSY'S SUPPORT of the Spokane International Railway in 1906 left little doubt that he meant to do serious business in the United States, including freight and passenger. He and his Soo Line counterpart, Edmund Pennington, immediately ordered six deluxe train sets and, in 1907, commenced first-class passenger service from St. Paul/Minneapolis to Spokane. The Soo-Spokane Train Deluxe attacked Great Northern in its heartland, instantly succeeding. It was initially designated as a seasonal service, but a press release at a reception in Spokane on October 17, 1907, announced the train would operate daily on a year-round schedule.

Soo-Spokane Train Deluxe, Fingal, ND, 1907. Photographer unknown. Courtesy Soo Line Historical and Technical Society Archives Collection.

Tail-end observation car, Soo-Spokane Train Deluxe, at Cranbrook History Centre, Cranbrook, BC. Photographer Terry Gainer.

According to the dispatch, W.G. Murphy, general travelling agent of the Canadian Pacific, addressed a group of Spokane area businessmen. "While it was the original plan to take off the Spokane Fast Train during the winter, the business has so far exceeded the anticipations that the officials of this company have decided to continue this service year-round."[1] Murphy further revealed the plan to extend the service to Portland, Oregon, partnering with the Oregon Railway & Navigation Line (a Union Pacific Company and another nemesis of JJ Hill's). The train was re-branded Soo Spokane Portland Train Deluxe.

The Soo and the CPR had stunned the railway world with their bold gamble, cracking Great Northern's supposedly unassailable monopoly in

1 *Cranbrook Herald*, October 17, 1907, courtesy Cranbrook History Centre, 57 Van Horne St. S., Cranbrook, BC.

Interior, tail-end observation car, Soo-Spokane Train Deluxe, at Cranbrook History Centre, Cranbrook, BC. Photographer Terry Gainer.

the Northwest. The Soo Line now had competitive access to the Pacific coast in the US, plus Vancouver, Canada.

The routing was Soo Line to Portal, CP's mainline to Medicine Hat, and the Crowsnest route to Cranbrook, connecting to Spokane International at Yahk, BC, to Spokane. The journey was marginally shorter than the Great Northern or the Northern Pacific mainlines, resulting in a competitive marketing edge. The quality and luxury of the train sets were unmatched, and they were the first in North America with electric lights.

To add insult to injury, in 1908, the Soo Line successfully lobbied the US government for the mail contract between the Twin Cities and Spokane. Shaughnessy and Pennington struck Hill and the Great Northern with a stunning blow; Hill was humiliated, adding to his hatred of the CPR that never wavered to his dying day. But one thing was unanimous. All parties agreed the train was a marvel for its day and, arguably, the most modern and well-equipped passenger train in North America.

In 1907, Barney & Smith Company delivered an order for six complete train sets, launching an all-new international service titled the Soo-Spokane Train Deluxe, a joint venture of the Canadian Pacific Railway and their US subsidiary, the Soo Line. This deluxe train linked the Twin Cities of Minneapolis & St. Paul with Spokane, Washington, the heart of the Inland Empire, travelling through western Canada instead of the mid-western states. Remarkably, the route was 10 miles shorter than the GN mainline and 40 miles less than the Northern Pacific mainline. The train was more than competitive, recognized as the premier passenger train in North America and the first train in North America with electric lighting throughout.

The tail-end cars were a wonder of craftsmanship and design. Beautifully proportioned and luxuriously outfitted, they graced the end of each train with their brass-railed open platforms, electrically lit domes, and coloured striped canopies. Each car's rear end had a new feature, an electrically illuminated circular tailboard sign spelling out Soo-Spokane Train Deluxe.

In each train set, ahead of the tail-end observation car with a library, buffet and four compartments, was a twelve-section, one-compart-ment sleeper, followed by the dining car, the first-class coach, the tourist sleeper, and the head-end mail-express-baggage car. The dining car was magnificent, with inlaid mahogany panelling, white tablecloths, sterling silverware and white-jacketed stewards providing outstanding service. Leading the consist was a fast and powerful 4-6-2 Pacific-type locomo-tive capable of maintaining a high-speed schedule. Overall, 36 railcars were built exclusively for this service, providing the six train sets required to operate daily.[2]

The company numbered all trains. Train #151, the Soo-Spokane-Portland Train Deluxe, departed St. Paul daily at 10:30 p.m. and Minneapolis at 11:10. A Sunday departure had you cross the border at Portal, ND, at 2:05 p.m., Monday, Cranbrook, BC, at 3:05 p.m. on Tuesday, Spokane that same

2 Terry Gainer, *When Trains Ruled the Kootenays: A Short History of Railways in Southeastern British Columbia* (Victoria, BC: Rocky Mountain Books, 2022), 60–61.

Soo-Spokane Train Deluxe at Cranbrook station, 1907. Photographer unknown.
Courtesy Cranbrook History Centre.

evening at 8:00 p.m., and Portland at 11:00 a.m., Wednesday. Train #150, the eastbound Soo-Spokane-Portland Train Deluxe, departed Portland daily at 9:00 p.m. A Sunday departure had you in Spokane at 3:00 p.m., Monday, Cranbrook at 10:30 p.m., Portal at 12:30 a.m., Wednesday, Minneapolis at 4:40 p.m., and St. Paul at 5:20.

In addition to the surging ridership from Chicago, St. Paul, and Minneapolis, the "local" market from Cranbrook and the Crowsnest mining communities eagerly awaited this classy and convenient train to Spokane. For years, British Columbians had been hungering for convenient access to the selection of cheaper and quality goods in the United States. The announcement of this new passenger train created immense excitement and became the event of the year in southeastern British Columbia and, surprisingly, southern Alberta. Before 1907, and the Soo-Spokane train, Spokane seemed to be a remote place for most Canadians. Then, suddenly, it was only a day away.

Throughout the spring and summer of 1907, the *Cranbrook Herald* had weekly updates on the Soo-Spokane, reporting the conductor allowed a walk-through of the first arrival on July 4, 1907, giving the townsfolk a taste of the travel experience to Spokane. It attracted hundreds and delayed the departure, but it was a public relations coup. The September 12, 1907, edition reported, "A lady passenger gave birth to a baby boy on the westbound train. Mother and child were doing well when they arrived in Cranbrook." Demand was beyond expectations; CP and the Soo Line had a winner.

But timing is everything. The outbreak of World War I, on July 28, 1914, prematurely ended the successful life of this innovative train. After the war, a similar schedule was available from the Twin Cities to Spokane, but it was not a dedicated train throughout the journey. Spokane-destined sleeping cars were available from the Twin Cities, switched onto the Kootenay Express at Medicine Hat, Alberta, and the Spokane International at Yahk, BC. The connections were quick, joining awaiting trains. However, into the 1920s, Spokane's importance as a major mining and financial centre began to fade as the mines in Idaho's Silver Valley and southern British Columbia petered out. The Soo-Spokane Train Deluxe was never to return. A few of the elegant cars owned by Canadian Pacific were integrated into the Imperial Limited, CP's crack transcontinental train. The remaining cars from the train deluxe became standard equipment on the Atlantic Limited, the Laker, and the Manitoba Express.

Tailboard sign courtesy Soo Line Historical and Technical Society Archives Collection.

CHAPTER 11

The Mountaineer

AFTER THE ARMISTICE WAS SIGNED on November 11, 1918, ending the Great War, the world was struggling with the return of millions of veterans. A peacetime economy had yet to find solid footing, and thousands were unemployed. Simultaneously, the war's end saw the Spanish flu pandemic rise. Business travel across the continent faded, and falling passenger numbers on the Soo Pacific had CP and Soo officials concerned. But as the economy surged with the Roaring Twenties, tourist travel numbers increased exponentially, leading Soo and CP executives to consider a summer-only tourist train to capitalize on the pent-up demand for leisure travel. CP's Grand Resorts of the Canadian Rockies and coastal cruises to Alaska, Victoria, and Seattle would be the hook.

On June 10, 1923, the Soo Line launched the Mountaineer, its finest and most successful passenger train, travelling a daily 2,200-mile, two-nation journey from Chicago to Vancouver, British Columbia. City stops included Milwaukee, St. Paul, and Minneapolis, with intermediate stops in rural Minnesota and North Dakota, crossing the border at Portal into Canada. The Mountaineer joined the Canadian Pacific mainline at Moose Jaw, Saskatchewan. After a second night on board, the Mountaineer arrived early morning in Banff, home of the famous Banff Springs Hotel, and mid-morning at Lake Louise station. A five-mile tramway transferred passengers to Chateau Lake Louise. Set on the shore of the lake, with the massive Victoria Glacier in the background, this vista was often referred to in railway publications as the eighth wonder of the world.

Crossing the Continental Divide, the Mountaineer descended into British Columbia via the Spiral Tunnels and Kicking Horse Pass to Field, BC. The train arrived in Revelstoke, BC, late afternoon after a spectacular journey. A third overnight delivered the passengers to Vancouver, arriving at 7:30 a.m. Passengers travelling onward for Victoria, Seattle, or Alaska boarded a stately Canadian Pacific Princess ship at the foot of Waterfront Station at Pier C. Porters were on hand to transfer all luggage to the vessel.

The eastbound Mountaineer departed Vancouver daily at 6:30 p.m. Both westbound and eastbound schedules passed through the Canadian Rockies in daylight, and both departures boasted open-air observation cars through the mountains. Departing Revelstoke at 7:20 a.m., the train summited the Columbia Mountains via Rogers Pass and the Rockies through Kicking Horse Pass. Passengers for Lake Louise disembarked in mid-afternoon; arrival in Banff was an hour later, a two-night journey back to the Twin Cities and Chicago from Banff.

The Soo Line spared no expense to equip the Mountaineer.

Among the last new passenger cars purchased by the Soo were four ob-servation-buffet-lounge cars. The cars contained an eight-seat solarium, a seventeen-seat observation room, a buffet kitchen, two smoking rooms and a women's lounge. A writing desk was placed next to the buffet. Much of the interior décor was natural walnut, the seats upholstered in striped mohair. Showers and bathrooms for men and women completed the amenities. The buffet, equipped with refrigerators, served ice cream and soft drinks. Canadian Pacific also constructed four similar cars for the Mountaineer consist.[1]

The first Mountaineer, powered by a 4-6-2 Pacific, departed Chicago leading a baggage car, two coaches, a 12-berth tourist sleeper, a dining car, two first-class sleepers, and an all-new tail-end observation car. The Mountaineer, launched with much fanfare and public relations, did not disappoint. The train was so successful that, by the mid-1920s, it often ran multiple sections. At its peak, eight extra sections departed over a week-end. To fulfill the demand, the Soo Line chartered Pullman sleepers and diners, including Pullman staff, a practice that continued throughout the lifetime of the Mountaineer.

----

1 Patrick Dorin, *The Soo Line* (Seattle: Superior Publishing Co., 1979).

Soo Line observation, buffet, lounge cars, c. 1929. Photographer Kaufmann and Fabry. Courtesy Soo Line Historical and Technical Society Archives Collection.

The Soo and the CPR captured a healthy market share of the upscale carriage trade on earlier trains to Canada. But the affluence of the 1920s created a middle class enjoying a level of disposable income affording the ability to travel. Coupled with inexpensive escorted package tours, it meant a new wave of American travellers took to the rails.

Packaged train tours date back to the 19th century. Thomas Cook, a cabinet maker and former Baptist preacher, is credited with founding modern tourism in Britain. In 1841 he persuaded the Midland Counties Railway Company to run a special train between Leicester and Loughborough for a temperance meeting on July 5. It was the first publicly advertised package excursion train in England. The round trip included a ham sandwich and a non-alcoholic beverage for the price of one shilling. Three years later, the railway agreed to make the arrangement permanent if Cook would provide passengers for the excursion trains. The business model, refined by introducing the hotel coupon in 1868, provided travellers with detachable coupons in a counterfoil book. These were valid for a restaurant meal or an overnight hotel stay, provided they were on Cook's list.[2]

Tour operators mushroomed in North America in the early 20th century; rail tours and cruises became the most desirable travel options. Brownell Travel is the oldest operating travel agency in the United States. In 1887, Walter A. Brownell founded Brownell Tours in Syracuse, New York, taking the first ten guests on an archeological tour of Switzerland. In 1900, Dr. George Brownell and his wife Jennie took over operations, and in 1946 Brownell opened a branch in Birmingham, Alabama, today's headquarters.[3]

Brownell was a substantial client of the Soo Line and the Mountaineer, packaging active adventures in the Canadian Rockies dating back to the early years of the Soo Pacific in the 1890s. I remember slinging bags for Brownell's numerous departures when I was a redcap at the Banff Station in the late '50s and early '60s.

The demand for leisure travel increased exponentially, spurred by brilliant promotions produced by the railways in the 1920s. Train tours to national parks and California were the "flavour of the day." Colourful posters of mountain hotels and trains with scenic backgrounds graced the stations and travel agencies. Canadian Pacific and the Soo Line were among the leaders, promoting CP's resorts in Canada's Banff, Yoho, and Kootenay national parks. Yellowstone National Park was primarily the baby of the Northern Pacific. The railway branded itself as "Yellowstone Park Line," feeding its investments in Old Faithful Lodge, Yellowstone Lake Lodge, and the National Hotel at Mammoth Hot Springs, later to become the Mammoth Hot Springs Hotel. Great Northern lobbied the US Congress to create Glacier National Park and created a network of accommodations, including Glacier Park Lodge, Lake McDonald Lodge, and Many Glacier Hotel, to compete with other national park destinations. Yosemite and Grand Canyon national parks became Southern Pacific's main tourism initiatives. In later years, Union Pacific jumped on the bandwagon,

----

2 "Thomas Cook: British Businessman," Britannica, https://www.britannica.com/biography/Thomas-Cook.

3 "History," Brownell, https://www.brownelltravel.com/about/history/.

building a rail line to West Yellowstone. Chicago, Burlington and Quincy followed suit with a rail line to Cody, Wyoming, utilizing Yellowstone's east entrance as its national park gateway. Building westward in the early 1900s, the Milwaukee Road realized the importance of tourism and a national park destination, developing its own Yellowstone resort called Gallatin Gateway.

The industry soon recognized another change in travel demands. The appeal of multifaceted itineraries quickly caught on. The Pacific Northwest plus Canadian Rockies itinerary offered by numerous tour operators was a classic example. Passengers travelled on Union Pacific, enjoying a two-night stay at the Sun Valley Lodge. Departing Sun Valley, the train arrived in Portland the following morning. In Portland, a two-day visit included a city tour before boarding Northern Pacific's morning departure to Tacoma. A motorcoach whisked the group on a day of sightseeing en route to their hotel in Mount Rainier National Park. After a morning tour to Seattle and Port Angeles, a ferry sailed the Strait of Juan de Fuca to Victoria, where passengers boarded Canadian Pacific's coastal liner, *Princess Marguerite*, to Vancouver. Docking at the foot of the Vancouver train station, passengers boarded the Mountaineer for Banff and the Canadian Rockies.

Other tour operators had similar itineraries, some to Los Angeles on the Santa Fe Railroad and up the coast to Seattle, or Great Northern to Glacier Park and Seattle. Cartan Travel Bureau, established in Chicago in 1899, had a different approach to a Rockies itinerary. Cartan travelled on Great Northern from Chicago to Winnipeg and Canadian National to Jasper Park Lodge, continuing to Vancouver. But like all itineraries visiting Vancouver, Cartan used the CP and Soo Line back to the Twin Cities and Chicago; the Mountaineer was the big winner!

Most railway agencies published colourful travel guidebooks. Increasingly through the 1920s, some publications were targeted explicitly at less urbane travellers of more average means, listing rail vacations and places of interest available to people of less extravagant tastes. But CP and the Soo Line focused on the carriage trade, which demanded first class! The top end of the carriage trade was little affected by the Depression, partially insulating the Banff Springs and Chateau Lake Louise from the coming apocalypse.

THIS IS A

CANADIAN ROCKIES
YEAR

Plan Your Vacation Itinerary
so as to use

The Mountaineer

$OO
LINE

THROUGH TRAIN FROM
Chicago
St. Paul
Minneapolis
TO
Banff

Lake Louise
Field
Glacier

Vancouver
Victoria [Can. Pac. / S. S. Line]
Seattle [Can. Pac. / S. S. Line]

Notes
BY THE WAY *to
the* PACIFIC COAST
Mountaineer
and CHICAGO ST. PAUL
MINNEAPOLIS
thru the CANADIAN
PACIFIC ROCKIES

Notes by the Way to the Pacific Coast, published by the Soo Line, c. 1924.
Courtesy Soo Line Historical and Technical Society Archives Collection.

Travel reached an all-time high in the summer of 1929, but the stock market collapsed in October. The year 1930 was worse, devastating the tourism industry. The Mountaineer operated through the 1930 summer season. However, the Depression arrived in full force, and most railways, including the Soo, severely cut services. System-wide decreases in passenger revenue hit 35 per cent in 1931–1932. In 1931, the Soo Line cancelled the Mountaineer, but the Canadian Rockies and Vancouver service continued as the Soo-Dominion. The through cars, including first-class and tourist-class sleepers and coaches, travelled on train #3 to Portal, North Dakota. A split section of the Dominion awaited, led by a CP locomotive to

Early season Mountaineer, Banff, 1947. Photographer Ron Duke. Courtesy Whyte Museum of the Canadian Rockies and Archives.

Moose Jaw, Saskatchewan. In Moose Jaw, a seamless switching manoeuvre joined the trains, and it proceeded west as the Dominion.[4]

In 1937, increased tourism demand saw the restoration of the Mountaineer, operating in July and August through the summer of 1941. That year, the United States entered World War II, and all nonessential services paused. The federal government assumed control of all railways in the US, concentrating on the war effort until 1944.

After the war, travel demand reawakened, and the Mountaineer was "back on the tracks" in 1947. Passengers returned in pre-Depression numbers. Canadian Pacific's Rockies resorts, closed during the war, reopened their doors for summer in 1946. All systems were "go," but the new and refurbished CP and Soo Line equipment had yet to come. The Pullman Company of Chicago provided most of the Mountaineer equipment in 1947.

....

4 The Mountaineer was a summer-only train, but the Soo-Dominion connection also operated in the spring, fall, and winter, from 1923 until 1963.

Throughout 1947, the Soo Line began a massive refurbishment of its equipment, opting to rebuild rather than purchase expensive stainless steel streamliner equipment. The Soo's "rebuilds" far surpassed the quality of the new streamliners. It proved to be a wise decision when train travel began to decline in the late '50s.

Soo upgraded the diners to gas-fired kitchens, eliminating coal and charcoal. New equipment, including refrigerators and dishwashers, highlighted the improvements. Reconfigured heavyweight sleepers accommodated the preference for more bedrooms and fewer sections. The observation buffet cars built in the 1920s were casualties of the war effort, replaced with the CPR's newly configured compartment observation lounge cars. In 1949, CP introduced its new flat-sided, semi-streamlined Grove series sleepers, another attractive upgrade to the Mountaineer equipment. The Grove equipment offered two models: one car set with four bedrooms and ten roomettes, the other with ten compartments, addressing the growing demand for more modern sleeping accommodations in the US market.

A 1947 westbound Mountaineer loading in Banff. Note the Pullmans and open-air observation car. Photographer Ron Duke. Courtesy Whyte Museum of the Canadian Rockies and Archives.

CP also renovated several heavyweight sleepers to align with the changes made by the Soo Line.

In the late 1940s, CP introduced the deluxe 2200 series Grove-style first-class day coaches. The new coaches were flat-sided and semi-streamlined with large windows and featured reclining seats, overhead luggage racks, hat racks, and mechanical air conditioning. In 1949, the new day coaches debuted on the Mountaineer and were immediately popular with budget tour operators.

A typical Mountaineer departure consisted of a single baggage car; at least two 2200 series day coaches; one ten-compartment Grove sleeper; one ten-roomette, five double-bedroom Grove sleeper; one refurbished heavy-weight with eight sections, one drawing room and two compartments; a rebuilt Soo dining club lounge car; and a refurbished heavyweight observation lounge sleeper with four double bedrooms and one compartment. An open-air observation car, added in Calgary, enhanced the journey through

A 1952 promotional shot of the Mountaineer at Morant's Curve. (Note the new flat-sided, semi-streamlined baggage car, coaches, and Grove cars.) Photographer Nicholas Morant. Courtesy Whyte Museum of the Canadian Rockies and Archives.

The second section of the eastbound Mountaineer awaits passengers from tour coaches at the Banff station, 1948. Photographer George Noble. Courtesy Whyte Museum of the Canadian Rockies and Archives.

the Rockies. Several Pullman sleepers and a Pullman diner completed the consist on most departures.

In 1950, Mr. G.A. MacNamara, the incoming Soo Line president, faced some difficult decisions as passenger train revenues tumbled. New highways, federal freeway construction, and automobiles were fast eroding intercity services, and many shorter passenger runs were no longer viable. Cost savings were the order of the day. Even the Mountaineer, the money-making darling of the system, experienced changes as MacNamara discontinued passenger service from Chicago. Passengers from Chicago and beyond now travelled with other railways to board the Mountaineer in St. Paul. Many veterans in the company feared a backlash despite the savings. But, as sometimes happens, the change was greeted positively.

The Chicago & North Western and the Milwaukee Road trains cut the travelling time to St. Paul, providing westbound passengers with later morning departures and more convenient arrival times in the Twin Cities. In addition, eastbound travellers from the Mountaineer enjoyed similar benefits, benefitting from the morning streamliners back to Chicago.

Through the mid '50s, the Mountaineer was on a roll, reversing the image of the money-losing passenger train that plagued most American railways. Often, the train ran with two, and sometimes three, sections a day throughout the season. For example, the Banff yard, usually packed with Pullmans, became a mini-village in summer. Many group tour operators used sleeping cars as hotel rooms during their Rockies stop. It was also a mustering yard for extra equipment – CP, Soo, and Pullman – required to meet summer demand, complete with a yard switch engine. During the Mountaineer season, the Pullman Company maintained a Banff office to coordinate staff and rail car dispatch. Two electricians and a maintenance man were full-time from mid-June to early September. Under the contract, the CPR provided cleaning and car washing services. The Banff station was like a separate town in the summer months, operating on a 24/7 basis.

CHAPTER 12

The Mystique of the Mountaineer

FEW TRAINS COULD OFFER THE MOUNTAINEER'S sense of adventure. Spectacular destinations offered romance and mystique. For example, the longest two-nation train in North America travelled over 2,600 miles from Chicago, crossing the Great Central Plains and through the famous Canadian Rockies to Vancouver. Unlimited adventure greeted the passengers at the renowned Banff Springs Hotel and Chateau Lake Louise. The famous Empress and Princess liners awaited at the CPR docks in Vancouver, cruising to Alaska, the South Pacific, or the mysterious destinations within Asia. In a way, it was the Soo Line's grand version of the Orient Express.

The equipment on the Mountaineer reflected the distinct "Soo Style," resulting from an early management decision to construct its passenger cars rather than lease Pullman-built cars. After emerging from bankruptcy in the late 1930s, the Soo policy was "refurbishment rather than purchase," leading to total rebuilds of classic heavyweight equipment. Refurbishments to the sleeping and dining cars, keeping abreast of the changing travel demands of an increasingly discerning public, resulted in more deluxe amenities and interiors than the new stainless steel streamliners offered. Similarly, Canadian Pacific rebuilt its fleet contribution to the Mountaineer in step with the Soo Line, including the Grove cars and heavyweight parlour/observation cars. The interiors were never less than first-class.

The Pullman equipment that became essential to the Mountaineer resulted from the train's success. As the momentum built through the 1920s, it was not unusual for the Soo to operate the second and third sections of the train to meet demand. Even though the green, heavyweight Pullmans gave the Mountaineer a hybrid appearance, the quality remained top shelf. The mix of equipment provided a unique identity for the two-nation train.

Pullman "McKeever" interior. Photographer Hugh Hemphill. Courtesy Texas Transportation Museum, San Antonio.

Pullman "McKeever." Photographer Hugh Hemphill. Courtesy Texas Transportation Museum, San Antonio.

The Roaring Twenties created the romance and mystique of the Mountaineer. The 1920s was a period of spiralling economic prosperity in the US, and life improved for most Americans. The United States had become a vast industrial nation fuelled by massive supplies of natural resources. But the main reasons for the economic boom were technological advances. Mass production pioneered by Henry Ford, electrification of the country, increased employment, and cheap credit created a pool of new consumers. New mass marketing techniques delivered the commercial messages.

Like a mouse at a cat's breakfast, the contradiction of the Roaring Twenties was Prohibition legislation, enacted as the temperance movement swept across North America. The 18th Amendment to the Constitution outlawed the production, sale, and transportation of liquors in the US, but the demand never went away. In Canada, Prohibition came earlier and ended earlier, and by the early 1920s, most provinces had repealed restrictions on the manufacture and consumption of alcohol. It was legal for Canadians to export alcohol, but it was illegal for Americans to import spirits. Creativity, therefore, ruled the day. "Speakeasies," usually owned by the Mob, blossomed, especially in larger cities like Chicago. Prohibition fuelled a wide-open market to slake the thirst of a whiskey-hungry American public.

Enterprising and bold Canadian distillers established depots near the border. The Bronfman family, of Seagram's fame, accounted for half of the distilled liquor illegally imported into the United States. Samuel Bronfman's operations, headquartered in Montreal, operated at other locations along the border, including southern Saskatchewan. In 1922, Bronfman lost his brother-in-law, gunned down gangland-style near Bienfait, Saskatchewan, only a few miles north of the international boundary near the Soo Line to Moose Jaw.

Al Capone, the "Don" of the Mob in Chicago, became a larger-than-life antihero. He controlled much of the illegal liquor trade in Chicago and supplied the "booze" for bars and speakeasies. Whether justified or not, the Mountaineer, originating in Chicago and travelling into Canada, was inevitably linked with liquor and fell under suspicion of transporting it for the Mob. The Soo's publicity department took the hype to the next level, setting a "speakeasy feel" first demonstrated by publicity photos launching the new 1923 service.

Soo Mountaineer "Flapper Gals." Creative photography for the Mountaineer launch, 1923. Photographer Kaufmann and Fabry. Courtesy Soo Line Historical and Technical Society Archives Collection.

For the 2021 winter edition of *The Soo* magazine, Alton Chermak wrote a stimulating article about the Moose Jaw Connection, where Soo passenger trains to Canada joined the Canadian Pacific mainline. The following are excerpts from Mr. Chermak's article:

> In recent years, an intriguing story has gained currency. It's a tale combining elements of the Prohibition era; the notoriety of Chicago gangsters, clandestine activities and faraway places. And the Soo Line. The setting is Moose Jaw, Saskatchewan, in the mid to late 1920s. Beneath

the city streets and commercial businesses is a network of tunnels, originally constructed to provide access for the maintenance of downtown hotels. The tunnels provided refuge for Chinese immigrants hiding from Canadian authorities and, as reported, as a conveyance for smuggling alcohol during the Prohibition era. The rediscovery of the tunnels in 1985 led to promoting them as a significant tourist attraction, renewing the region's history with bootlegging. It is accepted that geography gave Moose Jaw a location favourable for being a distribution center for liquor destined for the US, and some of the criminal elements were known to frequent the city.

Why was the Soo Line implicated? Moose Jaw is a sizeable city, an essential divisional point and junction on the Canadian Pacific Railway, and a gateway for freight traffic into the US. It was also a stopping point on the route of the Mountaineer, the prestigious passenger train operated by the Soo Line and Canadian Pacific between Chicago and Vancouver. In the 1920s, travelling any distance between the Windy City and Western Canada would likely have been on this well-known train. And one of the subterranean tunnels in Moose Jaw led to the Canadian Pacific Railway passenger station. Connect the dots.[1]

Chermak cites author Gord Steinke, who published a fictionalized work entitled *Mobsters & Rumrunners of Canada: Crossing the Line,* in which he recounts Sam Bronfman and Al Capone meeting in Bienfait in 1926 to work out a deal to increase the volume of whiskey being smuggled into the US, then travelling to Moose Jaw to make further arrangements. Steinke writes, "Capone boarded at the Northwest station in Chicago and stopped at Eau Claire…The date given for the train's arrival at Moose Jaw was July 1, 1926." He also characterized Moose Jaw as "a gangster's haven and became known as 'Little Chicago.'"[2]

In an interesting sidebar, the same issue of *The Soo* refers to an article, "Secrets from the Past Come to Life." It tells of a Soo business car that fell

....

1 Alton Chermak, "The Lore of the Mountaineer, the Soo Line & Al Capone," *The Soo* 43, no. 1 (Winter 2021): 30.

2 Gord Steinke, *Mobsters & Rumrunners of Canada: Crossing the Line* (Edmonton: Folklore Publishing, 2003), 32.

Soo Line business car #52, 1940, Waupaca, WI. Photographer Neil Torssell.
Courtesy Soo Line Historical and Technical Society Archives Collection.

into private hands in 1960. An online memoir from the custodian back in 2003 states, "Older business cars built during Prohibition days had a hidden compartment for booze. My boss bought business car number 52, used by Soo Line presidents. Ten years later, a retired Soo 'car man' visited San Diego and asked to see the car. In the master bedroom, he cocked a sconce lamp to the right and lifted a panel in the woodwork. A compartment hid old corked bottles of Three Feathers Bourbon. They had been there for many years. My boss was flabbergasted."[3]

The American public was increasingly captivated, no doubt with assistance from Hollywood, by a romantic notion of gangsters and how they attacked the unpopular Prohibition mandates. The Mountaineer undoubtedly benefitted from this strange notion of romance, adding to its mystique. Into the late 1950s, the Mountaineer continued to be a Soo Line success and was instrumental in placing the Canadian Rockies on the tourism map of North America.

....

3 "Secrets from the Past Come to Life," *The Soo* 43, no. 1 (Winter 2021): 31.

CHAPTER 13

The Depression and the Dirty Thirties

THE GREAT DEPRESSION of the late 1920s and the 1930s was the worst economic downturn in the Western world's history. Real estate and land values collapsed, factories laid off workers and many closed. With the loss of jobs and severe wage cuts, consumer spending evaporated. It was a domino effect sweeping across the country. As a result, almost every economic factor was depressed.

Stock prices began to decline in September 1929, and in mid-October, the rout began. Panic set in, and on October 24, Black Thursday, a record 12,894,650 shares were traded. Investment companies and leading bankers attempted to stabilize the market by buying up great blocks of stock, producing a moderate rally on Friday. The following Monday, the market fell, and stock prices collapsed on Black Tuesday. The New York Stock Exchange traded 16,410,030 shares in a single day. Billions of dollars evaporated, wiping out thousands of investors, and stock tickers ran hours behind because the machinery could not handle the trading volume.[1]

During the Roaring Twenties, wild speculation drove shares to many multiples beyond value. When the market peaked in 1929, cracks became apparent in the financial system. Production declined, unemployment raised its ugly head, and agricultural America faced strong headwinds, including an excess of large bank loans that could not be liquidated. A perfect storm was brewing.

The Soo Line's backyard of rural Minnesota and the Dakotas was particularly affected, and the troubles began years before the stock market

---

1 History.com Editors, "Stock Market Crash of 1929," HISTORY, https://www.history.com/topics/great-depression/1929-stock-market-crash.

collapse. Farmers and ranchers enjoyed unprecedented prices for wheat, beef, and other commodities during World War I. The surplus income fuelled demands for more land to increase production. As a result, the banks willingly doled out the cash. But then the chickens came home to roost. With wartime demand gone, agricultural prices fell, and a bushel of wheat slowly slipped below production costs.

In addition to falling demand and prices, an unprecedented drought struck in the 1920s. Initially, the "dry" limited crop production, stunted pasture growth, and cattle feed became prohibitive for producers every second or third year, resulting in the inability of many farmers to pay the interest on loans, let alone the principal. Concurrent with failing revenues, land taxes increased sharply, more than doubling by the early 1920s. With mortgages in default, banks foreclosed on the land. But now the banks were land-rich and cash-poor, unable to sell the land to other investors to restore cash reserves. As a result, panicked depositors could not withdraw their money from the banks. By 1923, 99 banks in North Dakota were out of business. Farmers had no other option but to walk away, penniless and disheartened.

In another blow to Soo's bottom line,

In 1932, the Wisconsin Central Railway failed to earn its fixed charges and operating expenses. As the owner of practically all of the WC's capital stock and large amounts of the bonds, the guarantor of obligations and the operator of properties, the Soo Line made advances to the WC of over $2,200,000 in 1932 alone to meet the deficits and continue operations. The Soo Line could no longer provide such funds in 1933 and served notice of its intention to discontinue operating the property unless it was furnished with the funds to meet the future deficits. But the Wisconsin Central was unable to provide the funds. In that situation, one of the Wisconsin Central bondholders obtained the appointment of a receiver with power, subject to the Court's approval, to provide the funds for continuing to operate the properties through the issue of the receiver's certificates. In addition, the receiver immediately agreed with the Soo Line that it should continue to operate the WC on his behalf and be reimbursed for future deficits out of the proceeds of the receiver's certificates.[2]

For a time, the Soo Line dodged the bullet.

Then the ultimate hammer fell. By 1929, the Great Plains began to experience the most devastating weather event in North American history. Abnormally hot and dry weather turned farmlands to dust and lakes into muddy sloughs. Extreme winds blew away the parched topsoil. During a decade labelled the "Dirty Thirties," black clouds of dirt filled the horizons, turning day into night. From the southern United States, Oklahoma in particular, up into Western Canada, the continent's interior became a dust bowl. Eight years of drought peaked in 1936, setting heat records that still stand today. During the Depression years, grain shipments plummeted.

To provide perspective, in 1915, the Soo Line shipped 83 million bushels of wheat. In comparison, only ten million bushels shipped in 1934, and, as a result, Soo Line deficits continued to swell. "By 1937, parent company Canadian Pacific had advanced over 29 million to cover Soo's obligations, at which point the CPR finally said 'uncle.' In December 1937, the Soo Line filed for bankruptcy. Under trusteeship, the Soo Line continued deficits from 1930 through 1943. Net income figures in 1944 revealed a profit of $1,038,308 (thanks in part to good grain harvests and World War II). This profit allowed for reorganization and renewal. The line's loan schedules were approved and agreed upon such that on September 1, 1944, a new corporation, the Minneapolis, St. Paul and Sault Ste. Marie Railroad, began operation of the Soo and the leased Wisconsin Central."[3]

The CPR's secret weapon was back "on track" and roared into the 1950s.

---

2 Dorin, *The Soo Line.*
3 Gjevre, *Saga of the Soo,* 25.

CHAPTER 14

My Mountaineer

WHEN OUR FAMILY MOVED TO BANFF, my father, FL (Frank) Gainer, was appointed station agent, and the position included a residence on the top floor of the depot. Our balcony, perched just feet above the platform, became my special viewing area. I had lots of trains to watch. In the 1940s and 1950s, Banff, located on the CP mainline, enjoyed four transcontinental passenger trains east and west daily and a fifth train in the summer months, the Mountaineer, a tourist special from Chicago, St. Paul, and Minneapolis. It captured my heart from day one.

On Saturday, July 24, 1948, my mom, sister Frances, and I travelled to Banff on the Dominion. Then, as the train approached the station, the excitement overwhelmed me. I bolted from my seat and barely waited for the conductor to lower the steps to disembark. I spotted Dad and my brother Fred waiting on the platform. We were finally all together again in this magical place called Banff.

Dad and Fred arrived in Banff a couple of weeks before the rest of the family. By the time I arrived on the scene, Fred had scoped out the premises and explored every nook and cranny in the station. That afternoon, Fred took me on a guided tour. We stalked through the building from the furnace room to the waiting room to the baggage room. When we arrived at the east end of the station, I couldn't believe my eyes! A complete train set sat in a siding adjacent to the mainline. I had never seen a full train so close up before. But, except for the majestic steam locomotive at the head end, it didn't look like a Canadian Pacific train. Most cars were painted olive green and labelled "Pullman." So I asked Fred, "What kind of a train is this?" He replied, "It's a train from America, and one like this comes every day." My 6-year-old curiosity took over. Except for the movies, I'd never

The Dominion arrives in Banff, 1948. Photographer George Noble. Courtesy Whyte Museum of the Canadian Rockies and Archives.

seen an American before. "Where are all the Americans?" I asked. "Oh, they are on buses sightseeing or something. They get on the train later," was Fred's reply.

I needed to get to the bottom of this, so the next day, after a hasty breakfast, I ran down to the east end sidings, called the Garden Tracks (parking tracks), so named because of the spectacular surrounding rock garden. But the train was gone. Dejected, I returned to the station, where I encountered a man in a conductor-style uniform. I asked him if he knew where the green train was. It took a minute for the "green train" reference to sink in, then he laughed and said, "The train left yesterday in the late afternoon for Chicago. You must be Frank Gainer's boy. Your dad said you might be looking for me." The man was Les Christianson, the Pullman agent in Banff. Les explained the "green cars" and this summer train to me. Over the years, he became my "American" mentor, and I spent hours quizzing Les about passenger rail services and life in the United States.

Les was a full-time employee of the Pullman Company based in Chicago. He was assigned to Banff every summer, overseeing the Pullman sleeping and dining car operation in Western Canada. It was a busy position. Every summer, hundreds of sleeping and dining car staff would arrive in Banff on the Pullmans, reassigned to tour groups returning to the Twin Cities and Chicago after their vacation on the west coast and the Canadian Rockies. Les was in charge of all logistics, including scheduling and ordering supplies.

Additionally, he had local hires to oversee, including two electricians and car maintenance personnel. Les also provided daily updates identifying the outgoing Pullmans for the switch crew and station master. The redcaps would load the assigned sleepers as the group luggage arrived at the station from the various hotels. Little did we know that I'd be one of the redcaps ten years later.

I quickly settled into a routine for the rest of the summer. My morning stop was the waiting room, checking out the passengers. It was a busy time, with two trains arriving only minutes apart. Train #2 from Vancouver arrived at 9:55 a.m. and departed for Calgary at 10:05. Some passengers were Banff residents going to the "big city" for the day. Still, most were awaiting the westbound Mountaineer's arrival, which eased into the platform at 10:15. The Mountaineer passengers were mainly Americans and immediately recognizable, always "dressed to the nines" for train travel.

The Garden Tracks were my second stop of the day. I met many sleeping car porters and dining car staff that rotated through Banff, often several times each month. This little kid had a million questions. I wanted to know all about the Pullman cars and the Mountaineer. There was also a method to my madness; often, the kitchen crew had a fresh-baked treat for the "kid."

Through the early 1950s, my life at the Banff station seemed like paradise. I had a real railway in my backyard and lived across the tracks from the "station bush," as we called it, with two creeks winding through the forest, teeming with fish. They were some of the best years of my life. But a few bumps popped up, and in late 1954 my 12-year-old world was shaken to the core when Dad announced he was retiring from the CPR. He had already dodged retirement at 65 with a two-year good health extension, but age 67 was the upper limit. I had never even entertained the idea we'd ever

Beyond the kiosk and the rock gardens are the Garden Tracks, with "extra" livery awaiting the Mountaineer, 1958. To the left, the Canadian has arrived. The redcap, lower left, is yours truly. Photographer Nicholas Morant. Courtesy David Fleming, Encyclopedia of Banff History.

have to move away from my kingdom at the station; it was like moving to another world.

In a way, it was. Then, in December, we moved into a duplex in town. It was much smaller than our home at the station; it didn't have a huge basement and furnace room where my brother and I had our model railroad. I could no longer wander downstairs in the evening to the telegraph office, sending telegrams and practising Morse code, nor could I visit with all the station employees I had taken for granted. I felt I no longer belonged to the station community. So I made a vow that, as soon as I was 15 years old (the minimum age requirement to work for CP back in the day), I'd get a job at the station.

Almost as if I were stalking them, I made frequent visits during the winter of 1956–1957 to Merle Sundberg, the baggage master, and Walter Richmond, the station agent. My mission was to drop hints about a job in the baggage room. Merle recommended me, and my application was approved. I was in seventh heaven. I was back at my beloved station!

So began my six summers working at the Banff station. I was a baggage porter for two seasons, checking luggage and loading the baggage cars. The baggage room opened at 8:00 a.m. to accept luggage checked through to the final destination. In 1957, train #13, the westbound Mountaineer, was the first train, arriving at 9:10 a.m. The Mountaineer had no head-end mail or express cars, just one baggage car, and on most arrivals, it would be packed with Banff-destined luggage. Passengers were allowed (and even encouraged) to check large items, such as steamer trunks, a day or two before their departure, ensuring they would be available at the destination. Why steamer trunks? A typical stay at the Banff Springs Hotel for well-heeled families could be two and three weeks, and formal evening wear was required. Or a family would venture from Banff to Vancouver, boarding an Empress liner to the South Pacific or Asia. Lots of formal clothing would be required!

Checked Banff luggage originating in the US was stored in a locked In-Bond room, as it had yet to clear customs. The Canadian government posted a customs officer in Banff during the summer season. It was a plum posting; it included accommodation and full meal service at the Banff Springs Hotel. When the passengers arrived, the customs officer would escort them to the In-Bond room and stamp the luggage tags as cleared. We'd then hustle the suitcases and trunks to the hotel's conveyance vehicle, and away it went. I can never recall the customs officer opening a bag to explore the belongings. But, as Fergy, one of the officers, explained, "These folks just don't do those sorts of things." The '50s were a different world.

One evening during my first season, I was the late man closing the baggage room. I was about to leave when the phone rang. It was Tom Egan, CP's passenger service representative. Tom asked me to keep the baggage room open until a couple arrived by taxi from the Banff Springs Hotel. They would be taking the last train of the day to Calgary. Train #6, the evening mail train, arrived at 7:10 p.m. but only had a day coach. There was no baggage car, as I explained to Tom. He said, "I know that, but I will ask you to be inventive." The couple was flying home to New York on a family emergency. Tom had refunded the Mountaineer train ticket and rebooked them by air from Calgary to New York. But the airlines were not going to accept all the luggage; they had one trunk and two large suitcases for a long-stay vacation in Banff. So my responsibility was to take care of their belongings and perhaps send them by CP Express the next day. As the mail train pulled into the station, a taxi arrived at the baggage room door, packed with bags. The couple was in a panic, so I led them through the baggage room to the platform and helped them board the day coach. I assured them I'd ship the luggage to New York. I gave them my name; they were probably skeptical, but they were without options.

After some thought, I decided to pretend the couple were travelling home by train, and I'd check the luggage through to Grand Central Station in New York. It would be much easier for me and cheaper for them. So I called Tom, told him my plan, and asked if he could mail them the luggage checks. But I would need the number of the cancelled ticket. When checking luggage, we consistently recorded the passenger's ticket number. He paused, then said, "What the heck? We'll deal with it later if there is any blowback." I can recall to this day the routing of the bags: "CP to Portal, Soo Line to St. Paul, CB & Q to Chicago and New York Central to Grand Central Station." The next day, the luggage departed on the eastbound Mountaineer.

Tom asked to see me in his office a few weeks later. "Uh, oh," I thought, expecting I might be in trouble. Instead, he handed me an envelope and told me to go ahead and open it. Inside was a thank-you card for looking after the luggage, and, as I opened it, something fell to the floor. The card contained a glowing thank-you message from the couple. Then I picked up the paper off the floor to discover it was a "Ben Franklin," a US hundred dollar bill. I was stunned; the amount represented two weeks' wages for me. Tom also told me not to worry about any blowback; the couple had sent a letter to Canadian Pacific's head office in Montreal commending our actions. Then Tom told me who the husband was; apparently, he was a member of some famous New York banking family. It meant little to me, but obviously they could afford the tip.

Before I was old enough to work, my goal was to be a redcap. My brother Fred had been a redcap since 1953, and his stories cemented my ambition to follow in his footsteps. (He was also my hero.) Then, in the spring of 1959, Baggage Master Merle Sundberg offered me the position. I had finally made it to the top of my world! A redcap position was one of Banff's most sought-after summer jobs, and I was "over the moon."

Three seasons as a redcap sealed my love affair with the Mountaineer. Part of it was monetary, no doubt; most tips came from handling tour group luggage. But the character of the Mountaineer made all the difference. All the passengers, along with the sleeping and dining car employees, were American. Like most pre-boomers, we were fascinated by all things American. After all, this was the train from the United States! So friendly, gregarious, and generous, most US visitors seemed less formal and more open than Canadian and overseas travellers, engaging in conversation without pretension. However, any "My Mountaineer" description would be incomplete without describing a day at the Banff station. It was a train buff's delight.

By 8:00 a.m. on a typical day in 1958, the activity level was intense. Hotel transfer buses, limos, and private cars disgorged their passengers for the arrival of the westbound Mountaineer. Baggage trucks were unloading the tour group luggage, and the redcaps spaced said luggage into the sleeper compartments of the Pullmans parked on the Garden Tracks. After checking their bags, passengers were gathered at the newsstand, drinking coffee, purchasing that last souvenir, or waiting under the covered platform.

When the luggage was on board, the yard locomotive connected to the Pullmans and repositioned the cars onto track 2, adjacent to the mainline. At 9:10, the Mountaineer eased into the depot. Due to the switching and servicing requirements, it had a more extended station stop than the other passenger trains.

As soon as arriving passengers disembarked, the yard crew "cut" the train, usually ahead of the Soo-CPR parlour car and the open-air observation car. Towing the two cars backward, a quick switch onto track 2 enabled a connection to the Pullmans. Back onto the mainline, the yard engine and crew joined the Pullmans, the parlour car, and the observation car to the rest of the train.

Meanwhile, the rest of the yard crew serviced the train, unloading massive 700-pound blocks of ice into the belly compartments of the sleepers to feed the air conditioning system and reloading the dining car refrigeration units with new ice. All switching manoeuvres and car icings were over and done in 15 minutes. These guys were incredible. It was poetry in motion to see them in action. Embarking passengers were then allowed to board, and the Mountaineer departed after a 20-minute stop at 9:30 a.m.

Throughout the 1950s, the Mountaineer often operated with two sections. But there were differences in the consist of the trains. The second section ran without the signature Soo-CP equipment. It was usually an all-Pullman sleeping car train with Pullman diners. The crew were all Pullman employees, and the clientele were folks travelling with a tour group. Ten or more tour companies could be on board, up to 40 passengers per group. Most of the sleeping cars contained 12 sections, each with an upper and lower berth, accommodating 24 passengers. For the exclusive tours, some all-compartment sleepers would be in the mix.

But, unlike with the regular westbound Mountaineer, the second-section arrivals seldom departed Banff on the same day. Instead, after disembarking the passengers, the head-end locomotive disconnected. The switch engine and crew then repositioned the train onto the Garden Tracks at the east end of the Banff station, connecting the Pullmans to the steam plant for heat. The cars were plugged into the 440-volt power boxes, lighting the cars and recharging the A/C batteries. The head-end diesel locomotives turned at the wye east of the station and returned to Calgary. There were no diesel servicing facilities in Banff.

After disembarking, the passengers boarded sightseeing coaches to tour Banff and Lake Louise; the more economical tours returned to the station in the late afternoon, as the sleeping car was their Banff "hotel" accommodation. The first-class tour groups proceeded to the luxury of the famous Banff Springs Hotel. After a second day of touring and exploring, the groups spent another overnight in Banff.

A diesel set arrived from Calgary early morning and rested on track 2, adjacent to the mainline. The switch crew pulled the Pullmans from the Garden Tracks and connected with the diesel power. Following the first section of the Mountaineer's departure, boarding was completed, and the second section left for Vancouver. The two-night stopover of a complete train was a regular occurrence during the peak summer season.

But not all second (and sometimes third) sections of the Mountaineer continued to Vancouver. Many dedicated Canadian Rockies itineraries included three or four nights in Banff and Lake Louise, followed by motorcoach sightseeing to Jasper. After a two-night stay in Jasper, the groups returned home, travelling on Canadian National to Winnipeg and the Soo Line or Great Northern to St. Paul. As a result, such special sections were only one-way and died in Banff, appearing financially less desirable for Soo and CP load factors. But there was a method to this apparent madness.

After World War II, cooperation developed between previously hostile and competitive railways. They began to recognize that the enemy of the future was the airlines. Cooperative bulk fares, offered across the continent, encouraged more group travel. The Great Western Circle and the Pacific Northwest/Canadian Rockies Circle were popular itineraries constructed from bulk fare offerings. Both itineraries originated in Chicago but benefitted Canadian Pacific and the Soo Line the most. Several participating railways were booked from Chicago to California, Portland, or Seattle, with stops in Yellowstone, Yosemite, Sun Valley, or Glacier national parks in the US. However, only one train travelled from Vancouver to the Canadian Rockies and Chicago. The eastbound Mountaineer benefitted from 100 per cent of the circle tour business.

Pacific Northwest and Canadian Rockies tour itinerary. Courtesy Terry Gainer collection.

Cartan Tours 1953 *Canadian Rockies Wonderland* itinerary brochure. Courtesy Terry Gainer collection.

The popularity of the itineraries created a massive imbalance in the flow of rail traffic from west to east, posing a problem in providing sufficient equipment. In the day, tour companies booked space well in advance, providing the railways with snapshots of the load factors. The equipment freed up on the one-way second sections to Banff and Vancouver became available for eastbound departures. The Soo Line promoted selected dates for additional one-way, westbound itineraries on the Mountaineer at competitive rates, providing surplus equipment for eastbound requirements. In addition to the Pullman equipment, CP sleepers were positioned on the Garden Tracks, deadheaded from Calgary to meet eastbound demands. Then, like a giant puzzle, the season slowly came together.

Itineraries from Chicago and the Twin Cities, offering westbound, nine-day vacations, departed Friday or Saturday, allowing the traveller to use only five vacation days, utilizing both weekends. The two-night

Vanderbilt Tours 1955 *California Pacific Northwest Canadian Rockies* brochure. Courtesy Terry Gainer collection.

journey to Banff meant the busiest trains arrived on Sunday or Monday. Sunday departures were heaviest for the 14-day itineraries, as arrival back home would be on a Friday night, allowing a weekend to reorganize before returning to the routine of life. As a result, Tuesday morning arrivals were also busy. The Garden Tracks were like a village with the station as the hub. Westbound arrivals were far less active on Wednesday, Thursday, Friday, and Saturday.

The Wednesday, Thursday, and Friday eastbound departures from Banff were incredibly busy. These were the days when the flood of traffic from the circle tours departed Banff for a weekend arrival in Minneapolis, St. Paul, or Chicago. A typical Wednesday or Friday departure could see eight to ten sleepers, a diner, and two deluxe day coaches added to the incoming Mountaineer, boarding over 300 group tour passengers. The three redcaps would space over 400 bags.

But Thursday's eastbound departures sometimes bordered on chaos. In the height of the season, the Mountaineer usually operated in two sections from Banff. Both would board simultaneously; passengers for the first section boarded from the station platform, and passengers for the second section loaded from the wooden walkway alongside Garden Track 1. Over 900 passengers were boarding between 3:00 and 3:50 p.m. on most Thursdays, and the amount of luggage to be loaded was stupendous. Both trains departed within minutes of each other at 4:00 p.m.

Train #14, the eastbound Mountaineer, begins the climb from Golden, BC, into Kicking Horse Pass. Photographer Nicholas Morant. Courtesy Whyte Museum of the Canadian Rockies and Archives.

I spent four seasons as a redcap, and my memories of the Thursday departures are still vivid. They were crazy days, sweaty work slinging hundreds of bags onto overhead luggage racks or spacing in compartments, always racing against the clock. But one day stands out above all others in my memory bank.

In late July 1960, a massive special train arrived in Banff, the Buffalo News Special, travelling as the second section of the Mountaineer. The Buffalo News, as did many companies in the '50s and '60s, offered perks to their employees, like in-house travel clubs, with attractively priced (sometimes subsidized) group tours for company vacations. Buffalo News partnered with the Eastman Kodak Company of Rochester, New York, employing over 75,000 workers, and sold out the special, offering a Pacific Northwest and the Canadian Rockies itinerary. The train had travelled on the Northern Pacific Railway to Yellowstone, to Seattle, and across the border to Vancouver. The train departed for the Canadian Rockies following a two-night stay in Vancouver. On arrival in Banff, the switch crew required Garden Tracks 1 and 2 to position the train. The passengers (and luggage) had disembarked from the train in Field, BC, travelling in sightseeing coaches to Emerald Lake and Takakkaw Falls before beginning a two-night stay at the Chateau Lake Louise.

The following day, the Buffalo News tour manager contacted Tom Egan, CP's passenger sales representative, informing him the luggage would begin arriving at the Banff station on Thursday morning, between 8:00 and 9:00 a.m. It was to be loaded and spaced in the appropriate sleeping cars. All luggage was tagged with names, car numbers and section, and roomette or compartment space. Tom then called a meeting with the redcaps, informing us to come to work earlier than usual and commence loading as soon as the bags arrived. Then he dropped the bomb: this would be the largest group CP Rail had ever handled – 500 people and 1,200 pieces of luggage. We were apprehensive. The three redcaps were a great team, but we'd never loaded an entire train before, especially one this size.

By 9:00 a.m., four jam-packed trucks had delivered the luggage from Chateau Lake Louise. We commenced loading the cars and worked nonstop between the other train arrivals. We also loaded 12 other tour groups departing on the regular section of the Mountaineer, another 400 bags.

Unsurprisingly, Murphy's Law kicked in; both Canadians were exceptionally busy that day, and it seemed impossible we'd get all the bags on board. But help unexpectedly arrived. About noon, our pal Clark made the mistake of dropping by the station for coffee. Immediately pressed into service, Clark spent the rest of his day loading bags. We were tired, stiff, and sore, but elated. The bag count for all tour groups on both sections of the Mountaineer was spot on, and we'd finished the task before the scheduled departure time.

However, the best news came when we pooled and split our tips at the end of the day. After paying off Clark for his help, Johnny, Jim, and I split $749.00. It was the busiest day we ever had, and in 1960 that was an absolute fortune! So, in early September, I was off to university, and my savings paid for tuition, books, and room and board. The redcap job was indeed a plum position!

I returned to my redcap duties in mid-June of 1961 for another season. Although we never experienced another Buffalo News Special, the Mountaineer, defying trends of declining passenger counts across the United States, had a bounce-back summer, exceeding the numbers of 1960. During the 1961 season, the hype from the tour escorts was about the 1962 Seattle World's Fair. Most tour operators planned increased departures through the Canadian Rockies en route to Seattle and the World's Fair. The year 1962 promised to be huge, and I returned for one last season.

But lurking in the background were signs of things to come. In the fall of 1961, the Soo and the CPR announced the cancellation of the Mountaineer, shocking the travel industry. Instead, a Soo-Dominion hybrid would operate through cars to the Rockies and Vancouver from St. Paul and Minneapolis via Winnipeg. The bean-counters appeared out of step with the travel industry.

Tour operators worldwide had embraced the fair, and requests for train space to the west coast spiked. The staggering increase in bookings indicated that the Soo-Dominion concept to the Rockies would not service the demand during the summer peak. The solution was to operate a dedicated service for one more season. But there was a difference. This *modified* Mountaineer ran as a second section of the Winnipeger to the mainline at Winnipeg, then as train #5 to Vancouver. But railway veterans continued to call the train "the Mountaineer," and all would be well for another season.

CHAPTER 15

1962, Triumph and Tragedy

THE CANADIAN ROCKIES experienced a banner year in 1962, sharing top billing with the decade's main event: the Seattle World's Fair. The fair was a record-setting success from opening day, April 21, attracting over ten million visitors before closing on October 21. Once again, the Soo Line and the CPR were primary beneficiaries. The summer was a blockbuster! The massive increase in travellers fed the CPR ferries from Seattle to Victoria to Vancouver, and the Mountaineer enjoyed a record summer season.

Before 1962, the travel volume on the Mountaineer followed definite ebbs and flows as designed by the tour operators to maximize vacation days with set weekend departure dates. But, that summer, established patterns went by the boards. As a result, every day became a peak day. Tour operators offered daily departures to meet demand. Surplus sleeping cars joined the olive-green, heavyweight Pullmans, pulled in from other railways. On any Mountaineer departure, orange sleepers from the Milwaukee Road, flat-sided sleepers from the New York Central, and stainless steel streamliners from the Burlington Route were not unusual.

The four sets of Garden Tracks in the Banff rail yard accommodated ten sleeping cars each. At the end of most days, the yard was full of passenger equipment, and two sections of the eastbound Mountaineer were a common occurrence. "Pullmanville" was full all summer, and the Mountaineer was back! Throughout 1961, rumours were flying regarding the future of passenger trains. But the rebound in numbers during the 1962 season had many of the Banff summer staff convinced all would be well in "Railwayville." Not only were we naive, we were sadly misinformed.

I often dropped into Tom Egan's office to chat. Tom was my champion. To use Hollywood lingo, he was tall, dark, and handsome, and a master at public relations. As a CP executive, he was also well connected. I had planned a grand adventure, departing in the fall, but during a visit, I mentioned to Tom that I might cut my overseas experience short and return for another summer. I reasoned, "The money I made this year was beyond any expectation, and I don't want to pass up another good season." His response rocked me. "Terry, don't even think about changing your plans. The decision has been made; the Mountaineer is history. The Soo Line and the CPR plan to exit the passenger service everywhere. It will all be gone in ten years."

In hindsight, perhaps I shouldn't have been surprised, but it was a bitter pill to swallow. My favourite train was history. It seemed ironic that the Mountaineer's busiest summer would be the last for this storied two-nation train.

CHAPTER 16

The End of an Era

IN 1950, G.A. MACNAMARA took over the reins as the Soo Line president. He faced difficult decisions regarding the future of passenger service, despite the success of the Laker, Winnipeger, and Mountaineer. Although MacNamara commissioned equipment rebuilds, introducing the popular dining club lounge cars, air-conditioned coaches, and roomette/compartment sleepers, the improvements could not halt the loss of passengers and resulting deficits. "The company lost $8,520,972 on passenger trains in 1952. The actual cost to the Soo was $13,265,188, as revenues from mail and express totalled $4,744,216. At the time, private automobiles carried nearly 85% of total intercity traffic; trains handled about 8%, buses 5% and airlines 2%."[1] Thus began the cuts to operating expenses and formal applications to abandon passenger services; the writing was on the wall. The branch line services were the first to go, and some intercity trains were cut back from daily service to six, and sometimes only three, schedules per week.

By the mid-1950s, American railways appeared unified to exit the passenger rail business. Most public sentiments were against the railways abandoning passenger service, even though the riders had moved on to other modes of transportation. The "use it or lose it" scenario didn't fit the collective opinion. The State Public Service Commissions would not support outright abandonment; that was too political. But they did allow the first steps of service cutbacks. Often accused of concerted efforts to discourage ridership, the railways eliminated sleepers and dining cars on many routes. Once fully committed to, the decision to abandon passenger service was like the downslope of a roller coaster; it just kept picking up

---

1 Dorin, *The Soo Line.*

speed. "By 1959, all passenger service on the Wisconsin Central was gone. That same spring, trains 5 and 6 between Minneapolis and Enderlin disappeared, and the company posted a notice to discontinue trains 7 and 8 between Minneapolis and Sault Ste. Marie. That marked the end of the famous Atlantic Limited that began service in 1884."[2]

The Winnipeger and the Mountaineer soldiered on into the early 1960s. In 1962, the Mountaineer was rerouted through Winnipeg, joining the Dominion to the Rockies and Vancouver. But the exponential demand for train space due to the popularity of the Seattle World's Fair required a dedicated train for the entire journey. The Mountaineer survived one last season. In 1963, Banff and Vancouver equipment travelled the Winnipeger and the Dominion. But, by 1964, all reference to the Mountaineer had disappeared from the timetables. Like the Atlantic Limited, without any fanfare, it faded into history.

In 1964, the Soo Line, for the second time, petitioned to discontinue the Winnipeger. It was hemorrhaging financially, and cost cuts reduced the consist to one coach, a sleeper, and a baggage car. Dining car service was limited to the summer months. In 1965, the post office discontinued the mail service, and in 1966 the express commitment was cancelled. The loss of the contracts was a significant revenue setback. Finally, in 1967, the Soo Line received permission to exit the service, and the Winnipeger made her last run on March 25, 1967. The last of the Soo Line's "Famous Trains to Canada" quietly disappeared. Sadly, there were no curtain calls.

2 Dorin.

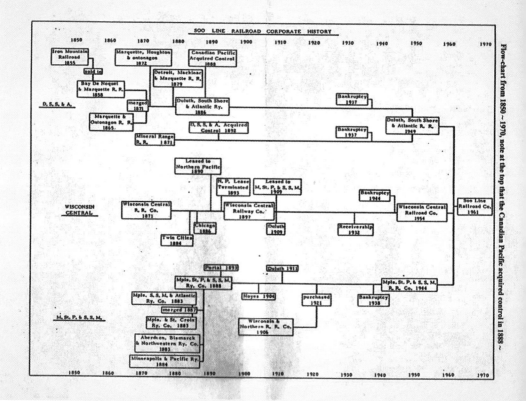

The corporate history of the Soo Line to 1961. Courtesy Soo Line Historical and Technical Society Archives Collection.

☙ EPILOGUE ❧

FOR 80 YEARS, the Soo Line passenger trains transported more Americans to Canada than any other railway. The Soo was "the little railway that could."

In railway terminology, the term *Varnish* referred to the gleaming teak and mahogany panelling of the wooden sleeping and observation cars constructed in the early days of passenger trains. As the passenger trains became more deluxe, the term evolved to describe the elegant first-class trains criss-crossing North America. During the first 60 years of the 20th century, Soo Line Varnish carried hundreds of thousands of visitors and tourists from Chicago and the Twin Cities to points across Canada. Destinations included Banff, Lake Louise, the Kootenays, Vancouver, Ottawa, Montreal, and the Maritimes. The famous trains connected with Canadian Pacific's luxury liners that spanned the world.

The first famous Soo Line Varnish, the Montreal-Boston Express, was later renamed the Atlantic Limited. The service began in the 1890s and prospered through the 1930s until being derailed by World War II. The Soo Pacific Express commenced operations in 1893 and, through various reincarnations as the Soo-Dominion, operated until 1964. The Soo-Spokane Train Deluxe followed in 1907, travelling through the Crowsnest Pass and the Kootenays en route to Spokane and Portland. The Winnipeger, inaugurated in 1894 as the Manitoba Express, enjoyed a 63-year run and was the last of Soo Line's Varnish. And the pride of the Varnish, the Mountaineer, enjoyed almost 40 years as Soo's premier passenger service. Indeed, the Soo had been Canadian Pacific's secret weapon during the golden age of passenger trains.

The transition to a dedicated freight railway was eminently successful. Once it was freed of the massive losses of the declining passenger services, and the conversion to dieselization was completed, the bottom line turned black. The Soo Line was "back on track."

In January of 1961, the merger of the Minneapolis, St. Paul and Sault Ste. Marie, the Duluth, South Shore & Atlantic, and the Wisconsin Central created a new entity called Soo Line Railroad Company. G.A. MacNamara, the former Soo Line president, became chairman of the board and Leonard Murray, previously president of the DSS&A, was appointed president of the merged lines. The new company reported a profit in its first year, and the Soo Line Railroad never looked back. Improvements that year included expansion of the Central Track Control beyond Minneapolis, a Shoreham yard upgrade to serve longer trains, and more 'in and out' tracks allowing better blocking of trains to increase overall utilization. By 1968, 1,360 new freight cars had joined the Soo Lines fleet, augmented by 1,150 high-capacity covered grain hoppers. In 1969, the Soo spent $5,700,000 for an additional 374 freight cars and ten EDM SD-40, 3000 horsepower locomotives at $250,000 each. By 1971, the 'New Soo' had spent over $100 million on improvements. Profits rose steadily, and in 1980, the railroad set a new high in revenues, with net income of $34 million, a 23% increase over the previous year.[1]

By the late 1980s, as the major shareholder, Canadian Pacific had become heavily involved in Soo Line operations and, in 1989, bought up all remaining stock, assuming 100 per cent ownership. In 1994, all identification became Canadian Pacific, and while the Soo Line name still exists, it is only a legal entity. The public identity is no more.

Yet the body of the Soo Line remains the heart of Canadian Pacific's operations in the US. With the recent Canadian Pacific and Kansas City Southern merger, the Soo Line empire links Canada, the United States, and Mexico. So, yes, Canadian Pacific's secret weapon lives on!

1 Gjevre, *Saga of the Soo*, 36–37.

❧ SELECTED SOURCES ❧

Abbey, Wallace W. *The Little Jewel: Soo Line Railroad and the Locomotives That Make It Go*. Pueblo, CO: Pinon Productions, 1984.

Chermak, Alton. "The Lore of the Mountaineer, the Soo Line & Al Capone," *The Soo* 43, no. 1 (Winter 2021): 30–33.

Dorin, Patrick. *The Soo Line*. Seattle: Superior Publishing Co., 1979.

Gjevre, John A. *Saga of the Soo: East, West and to the North*. Vol. 3. Moorhead, MN: Agassiz Publications, 2006.

———. *Three Generations West: Saga of the Soo*. Vol. 2. Moorhead, MN: Agassiz Publications, 1995.

Hudson, John C. "North Dakota's Railway War of 1905." Minneapolis: University of Minnesota Printing Services, 1981.

Larson, Robert. *Soo Line Remembered: A Scrapbook of Lifetime Memories*. La Miranda, CA: Four Ways West Publications, 2014.

Robinson, Bart. *Banff Springs: The Story of a Hotel*. Banff: Summerthought Publishing, 1973.

Sadis, Stephen, dir. *The Empire Builder: James J. Hill and the Great Northern Railway*. Documentary. Seattle: Great Northern Filmworks, 2022.

Soo Line Historical and Technical Society Archives. "Timetable Information 1889, 1894, 1903, 1906, 1907, 1923." http://www.slarchives@att.net.

State Historical Society of North Dakota. "The Great Depression and the Drought." https://www.history.nd.gov/textbook/unit6_1_docsimages.html.

Steinke, Gord. *Mobsters & Rumrunners of Canada: Crossing the Line*. Edmonton: Folklore Publishing, 2003.

Suprey, Leslie V. *Steam Trains of the Soo*. Mora, MN: B&W Printers & Publishers, 1962.

Wikipedia. "CP Ships." https://en.wikipedia.org/wiki/CP_Ships.

❦ ABOUT THE AUTHOR ❧

TERRY GAINER'S FAMILY arrived in Banff in 1948 when his father, Frank Gainer, was transferred there as station agent. From their arrival until 1955, the family lived in the residence atop the station itself. During those years, Terry explored every nook and cranny of the station and the surrounding grounds. From 1957, he worked summer jobs there, initially as a porter in the baggage room and then as a redcap through to the summer of 1962. This was the bonanza year of the Seattle World's Fair and the opening of the Trans-Canada Highway, but unfortunately also the beginning of the end of train travel to Banff. Largely influenced by his upbringing, Terry has enjoyed a career that has been an amazing 50-year adventure in tourism. Though he retired in 2005, he has stayed involved in the industry as a marketing consultant. In addition to *The Soo Line's Famous Trains to Canada*, Terry's books include *When Trains Ruled the Kootenays: A Short History of Railways in Southeastern British Columbia* and *When Trains Ruled the Rockies: My Life at the Banff Railway Station*. Terry lives in Nelson, British Columbia.